JUNIOR HANDLING

FELIX COSME

To the memory of
Joe Cartledge
who has done so much
for the advancement of
the junior handler

Published by Ringpress Books 1990
Spirella House, Bridge Road,
Letchworth, Herts, SG6 4ET

Printed in Great Britain
by The Bath Press

ISBN 0 948955 51 1

ACKNOWLEDGEMENTS

I would like to thank all the junior handlers who have provided information and photographs. Thanks also to Vince Mitchell, Marita Rodgers and Carolyn Whitlock. Plus a very special thank you to Joyce Collis, my friend and mentor since 1968, who has made this book possible, as well as many of the other things I have achieved in the show world.

CONTENTS

FOREWORD

Agreeing to write a Foreword for this book about a year ago is one thing – I am full of promises and good intentions – getting around to doing it is quite another. I am lucky that it is Felix Cosme who has written the book, as he is the most patient and understanding man I have ever met. At various times, he has gently reminded me that the deadline is approaching, but at no time has he ever got the slightest bit flustered about my lack of response. This is one of the reasons why Felix is ideally suited to be the author of this book, based on his own experiences and general advice to "budding" junior handlers. To be a successful handler you need to have endless patience and understanding, as well as a natural affinity with animals. I know I am not exaggerating when I say that Felix possesses all these qualities in large measures. I have known him for a long time – he used to handle dogs in the United States, where dog showing is a serious business, very competitive and ultra-professional. I recall him showing many of his partner's (Mrs Joyce Collis) Bearded Collies, and he has done much to put Border Collies on the map in the Best In Show rings, when the breed first gained full recognition and started to appear in numbers.

Felix has shown a keen interest in junior handling, and its progress, for almost as long as I have, and over the years he has given me invaluable advice and support. He has that rare quality of being able to gather a group of youngsters around him and talk to them at their own level. Although quietly spoken, Felix can still hold his audience completely captive. No questions would ever appear silly to him, and with his gentle ways he would be able to put the most shy and awkward beginner at ease. This book comprehensively deals with every aspect of junior handling, without getting too complicated or technical, and I see that it is going to become a "must" for all young dog people to read the book. And perhaps not just juniors involved with handling and showing dogs – Felix could teach most of us a thing or two!

Junior handling, or for that matter any kind of handling dogs, is not just about competing and winning – being a good winner is easy; being a good loser is a different matter altogether. Felix takes his readers through all the various stages. When guidance and advice are based on personal experiences and achievements, they are so much more valuable than something just copied out of a text book, and in Felix's case he has certainly done it all the hard way – from a nervous novice exhibitor to a very accomplished "professional" – and he has still managed to stay charmingly modest! A book of this kind has been badly needed for quite a while – the youngsters today are hungry for knowledge, but it is important that they are fed the right kind of knowledge – and they will certainly find it all in this book.

Liz Cartledge
Chief Organiser and Secretary
of the Junior Handling Association

Navy Days in Haiti: I am sitting on the left.

INTRODUCTION

From the first moment I could speak, I wanted a dog of my own. Many children long to have a dog, but in my case it seemed a hopeless ambition. My father died when I was only a baby, and my mother was left to bring up the family on her own. We lived in a block of flats in the New York ghetto of Spanish Harlem in the United States, and we were very poor. Like most of the families in that neighbourhood we had to fight for survival. A family pet would have been an impossible luxury. When I had the money, I spent all my free time at the movies. My hero was the famous Rin Tin Tin, a German Shepherd Dog, who performed magnificent feats of courage, and was also a loving companion. I dreamed of owning a dog like that. But when I eventually got my first dog, it was very different. Beauty was a cross-bred White West Highland Terrier type, and although I had fun playing with her in Central Park, she was not the brave and beautiful animal that I had longed for. She died after chewing an electric wire in our flat, and after that I abandoned all ideas of owning a dog. I went to Maritime School and joined the U.S. Navy when I was eighteen years old.

I enjoyed my time as a sailor and I had the chance to see many different countries. I also got married and had my own family. I had one year of duty in Vietnam, the country in the Far East which was then at war with America, and then I was ordered to join the U.S. Navy based in England. I did not want to come to

England at all; any other country in the world would have suited me better. I had heard about the terrible weather, and as I had married a Spanish girl, my sights were set on sunny Spain. Little did I realise that this was the turning-point in my life. All this time, I had cherished my ambition of owning a German Shepherd Dog, and when I was settled in a small village near High Wycombe, I got in touch with a lady advertising German Shepherd puppies. Like a real novice, I made no enquires and I dashed along to buy a bitch puppy from the litter. I called her Lady Demetrius, and although she had many qualities, it soon became obvious that she was not good enough to show. Her markings were correct, but she was slightly lacking in rear angulation and she was rather masculine in appearance. I lavished love and attention on her, and so she always looked in peak condition. She could not be a show dog, but she was a marvellous family pet and guard. We walked miles together and I was proud of my first pedigree dog.

I took her to the obedience training club in High Wycombe and this was my first taste of the competitive side of the dog world. I loved it, and soon I was involved in Ring Craft classes, designed to teach handlers how to show their dogs. My whole life revolved round the dog scene. I was attending three training sessions a week and competing in matches and Exemption Shows at every opportunity. I used to take Lady to the U.S. Base with me every day so that I could train her and exercise her during my lunch hour, and soon I felt ready to exhibit in Open Shows, although the thought of competing against the top handlers gave me butterflies in my stomach! There is a great deal you can learn from watching the experts, and I used to take a cine film of the handlers I most admired so I could study their technique. Then I would practise with my own bitch and get someone to take a cine film of me. I would then watch this over and over again to see where I was going wrong. There were three handlers that I particularly admired. Marjory Williams was a very confident and calm handler. She could control the most boisterous dog by using a fine choke chain and holding it just behind the dog's right ear. She would give the dog constant reassurance, using hand contact – and watching her move a dog with flowing, co-ordinated and rhythmic movement was a joy. Edwin White put so much effort

I handled German Shepherd Dogs in the States.

into handling a German Shepherd dog that he would perspire constantly in the ring. He had the ability to manipulate a dog, and could stack it and pose it in such a way that any dog would have looked elegant. Johnny Stokes was also very confident and competent, and I chose to copy his particular mannerisms. He saw the ring as a stage, and it was his job to perform. When the judge asked Johnny to move his dog, he would stand tall, get the dog's attention and then point it in the direction he wanted the dog to go in. He had so much charisma that all eyes around the ring would be concentrating on his every move.

I studied these three handlers so closely that I could just close my eyes and envisage the way each one of them handled a dog. But I knew it was not enough just to copy them – I had to develop my own style. I could not move as they did, because no two people move alike. I instinctively had a good sense of rhythm and balance, and so I was able to gait at any speed with well co-ordinated movement. I also mastered the art of quickly drawing a dog into what appeared like an effortless pose. The hardest part of my development was achieving calmness and control. This can only come from experience – constantly competing in a show ring and learning to ignore all the noise and distractions. You have to feel like you are on a raft marooned in the middle of the sea. The big test came when I was asked to handle a quality German Shepherd, Ritz of Hanslor, at the Alsatian Club Show. The judge was a breed specialist, and to my great joy I won the class, and was placed in front of Marjory Williams. I was now confident with German Shepherd Dogs, but I was not keen to handle other breeds. I was asked to handle a Beagle at the Hitchin and District Canine Society, so I made sure I was the last to be seen, to give me a chance to watch how the other handlers showed their dogs. I found it very strange to see them working on the dog's tail so that it would be held stiff and upright. Beagles are usually shown on a table, which I was not used to, so I had to bend double to pose the little dog on the ground. We were placed third, and it was a very useful experience for me.

After three years, I was due to return to the United States. I left Lady with a breeder to be mated to Ritz of Hanslor, and then she was to be sent to me in whelp. Tragically, Lady escaped from the kennels and was killed by a train. It was a terrible blow to me and to my family. Back in the States, I continued my involvement in the dog world, competing in shows and improving my style. Then fate took a hand in the advance of my handling career. I was looking for a high-quality dog to campaign. Ann Lenox had a beautiful German Shepherd Dog and she needed a handler. Fortunately we met, and I agreed to take the dog on. This proved to be no easy matter, for Lenoxhill Viking Pride was a shy dog that lived in a world of fear. Ann was devoted to him, and I think she had tended to over-protect him. As a result, I had to try to win the dog's confidence. I took him for long walks and then I started to train him. Gradually his confidence grew and we became very attached to each other. The big test came when we entered the Northern New Jersey German Shepherd Dog Club Show. I felt good, and Pride was relaxed and happy. To my great delight, we won Best in Show and we were presented with a large trophy. In all the excitement, I forgot to steady Pride and reassure him when the photos were being taken with the judge. Pride's fear came back and he backed off from the judge. The judge said that he had noticed the nervous look in the dog's eyes when he was going over him in the show ring, but he had been impressed by the way the dog had stood his ground. The lapse when the photo was being taken was entirely my fault. It was unforgivable to forget how the dog might be feeling. I blamed myself, but more importantly, I had learned a lesson, and I made sure it never happened again.

I applied for a professional handler's licence for German Shepherd Dogs, and at the same time I persuaded my Commanding Officer to let me enrol for a three-month course at the U.S. Air Force Patrol Dog School in Texas. This was the place where dogs were trained for sentry and drug detection duties. I was separated from my home and family, and so I gave most of my affection to Roscoe, the dog that was assigned to me. Thanks to the obedience training I had done in England, I was able to follow all the basic commands, and soon I developed a strong working relationship with the dog. Before I graduated as an honours student, I had the opportunity to join the drug detection class. On one occasion we had to find some granules of marijuana in an aspirin bottle buried in a flower bed in the entrance of a cinema. The cinema was empty, but the smell of the audience would still have been powerful to a dog's sensitive nose. Even so, the dog had no difficulty in finding the bottle. On another occasion there were two deposits of marijuana; one in a desk and one taped behind a picture. He found the first deposit, but he realised there was more to find, and after a good deal of sniffing, he switched his attentions from ground level and eventually found the second supply.

Shortly afterwards I retired from the Navy, and I received my professional handler's licence, but I could not find enough work to make a living. I was employed as a car salesman for four years and then, as my marriage had ended, I decided to make my home in England. I went into partnership with Joyce Collis and started handling Bearded Collies. This was certainly a new challenge, and I felt under a lot of pressure, particularly when my friends in

When I moved to Britain, I started handling Bearded Collies.

German Shepherd Dogs tried to make fun of me at the ringside. But soon the Bearded Collie exhibitors accepted the American professional handler in their midst, and some even tried to copy my style of handling the breed. I used to stand on the dog's right-hand side and hold the choke chain high on the dog's neck, just behind the ears. Then, with my right hand, I would walk the dog into a pose. I would make sure that the dog's front legs were parallel to each other, and then adjust the rear legs so that they were at least three inches behind the croup when looking down on the dog's rear. Once this was done, I would stroke the dog's coat with my open palm, adjusting the coat so it would lie close to the dog's body, but also giving reassurance without needing to speak. In fact, I very rarely talk to any of my dogs when I am showing them, other than to settle them or to encourage them to pick up the pace a bit.

When Joyce Collis was invited to judge abroad, I often accompanied her to give a display of handling skills. I did this in Denmark and Finland, and in 1980 I was asked to judge Junior Handlers in the United States. This was my first official association with the juniors. My involvement stepped up three years later when Liz Cartledge asked me to judge one of the classes at the semi-finals of the junior handlers contest at the Richmond Championship Show. It was at this point that I had to decide which direction I wanted to go in. My main strength was as a handler, and it seemed right that I should get involved in teaching youngsters. I decided to accept the judging appointment, and ever since then my aim has been to give junior handlers the help I would have welcomed so much during my childhood in Spanish Harlem.

Chapter One

THE START OF IT ALL

The first classes for Junior Handlers were held in the United States at the Westbury Kennel Club Show in Long Island, New York, in 1932. In those early days it was the cute children handling unruly dogs who usually won. The judges did not know what they were looking for, and toffees and chocolates were given to all competitors. It was not until 1971 that Junior Showmanship, as it is called in the States, received official recognition and rules and regulations were standardized. It has now become an important part of every dog show held in America, and the finals of the annual Junior Showmanship competition are one of the highlights of the Westminster Dog Show in New York, which is the equivalent of the British Crufts.

It was Joe Cartledge who was responsible for introducing junior handling to Britain. He had a dream of establishing a Dog Centre – a venue which would stage all types of competitions, and would also act as a training ground for youngsters. He set up an organisation, with his Swedish-born wife Liz, called the Dog Centre, and one of the events they organised was a trip to the Westminster Dog Show in New York. It was as a result of seeing

Joe Cartledge (second left) introduced junior handling to Britain.

the Junior Showmanship finals that Joe became increasingly interested in staging a similar competition in Britain. The Dog Centre therefore asked all Breed Clubs to put on two classes at their shows to be called the Dog Centre Junior Handling classes. These were to be split between two age groups – six-to-eleven years old and twelve-to-sixteen years old. The Dog Centre provided rosettes, and the winners of each class qualified for the semi-finals of the Junior Handler of the Year competition. The Dog Centre held its annual show on Cheltenham Racecourse and so this became the first home of the junior handling semi-finals and final.

In these early days there were no hard and fast rules as to how the classes were run; there was no specified prize money and the clubs were left to choose their own judges. The Dog Centre tried to encourage them to select judges with the experience and interest to help the youngsters, and they hoped the senior members of the club would also play a part in their training. When a junior qualified for the semi-finals they had to become a member of the Dog Centre Limited, which cost £1 per annum. The winner of the final was taken to the Westminster Show in New York, and the runner-up went to the Winners Show in Amsterdam.

Sadly the idea of building a Dog Centre in Britain failed to come to fruition, but the one thing that did survive was the format for a Junior Handling competition. The Junior Handling Association was set up and was supported by the Richmond Championship Show and Ryslip Group Limited. A controlling committee was formed consisting of Group Captain Sutton, Mrs Catherine Sutton, and Joe and Liz Cartledge. And from 1977 the semi-finals and final of the Junior Handler of the Year were staged at Ascot Racecourse in September, in conjunction with the Richmond Championship Show. The numbers of entries were increasing every year, and ultimately it was decided that Exemption Shows could no longer hold qualifying classes for the semi-finals.

Financially, the Junior Handling Association was holding its own, but it was a great boost when Pedigree Petfoods became involved in sponsorship. As a result, the final of the Junior Handler of the year was moved to join forces with Pedigree Petfoods Champion and Veteran Stakes, held at the Metropole Hotel near Birmingham over a weekend in January.

The prizes also changed as the expense, plus the close proximity of the Westminster Show and Crufts, made the trip impractical. As an alternative, visits to international dog shows in Europe were organised, and in 1989 the winner was taken to the World Show at Copenhagen. Winners were also offered the option of a pedigree puppy, and in recent years Tracey Alexander, the Bichon handler, bought a show puppy of her chosen breed.

Joe Cartledge became ill in 1981 and he finally lost his battle against cancer in December 1982, but his wife Liz has carried on the work of the Junior Handling Association and is now the secretary and chief organiser.

"The whole concept of junior handling was Joe's," she said. "It was his baby and he watched it grow from very humble beginnings to become a serious and very important part of dog shows. At one stage he was struggling to make a career as a professional handler, and he therefore understood all aspects of handling.

"When he died it was a great loss to me, naturally, but also to the world of dogs. The juniors lost a great supporter and friend, and I was left to take over as secretary of the JHA. It is a lot of hard work, but I find it very rewarding and I enjoy getting to know the juniors."

To begin with, the International Junior Handler of the Year final was held in Birmingham with representatives from the Scandinavian countries joining the British winners. But as interest in junior handling grew, it was moved to Crufts. It now has a truly international flavour, with some eighteen countries taking part and representatives coming from as far afield as Australia, New Zealand and the USA.

Chapter Two

FIRST STEPS

A lot of youngsters first become interested in junior handling because their parents are involved in the show world. Most will have grown up with pedigree dogs and will be used to going to shows with their parents. The most important first step is to watch the professionals handling their dogs, and then try to copy them when you are at home. To begin with, it is simply a matter of putting your dog on a lead and walking it round the garden. Then you can try and pose the dog. This is a stage where parents can be very useful, lending help and encouragement.

Over the years I have devised a sequence of exercises to help youngsters learn how to pose their dogs. I number the exercises, rather than shouting out instructions, which can be confusing and make the novice handler feel nervous. The ideal number to teach is a class of six children, as then you can give plenty of individual attention and encouragement. I also like to inject a bit of humour into the proceedings so the children do not feel under too much pressure. The most important aspect of the exercises is for the handler to learn how to control the dog. Sarah Court, aged eight, worked with me to show how the basic exercises should be performed. I asked Sarah to move the dog around a makeshift ring and then stop, for me to examine it. She moved off in a straight line and as she came back towards me, I told her to stop, approximately two metres from where I was standing. I told her to stand beside the dog and hold the lead in her left hand, and then to extend her right hand, palm upwards, and place it under the dog's jaw. She should hold it as though the dog's jaw was resting on her palm. Sarah had to repeat this exercise over and over again, until she had got it to perfection. The next step was to slide her right hand towards the dog's collar and gently exert control over the dog by holding its collar. We were then ready to move the dog. Sarah set off on the first leg of the triangle and when she was ready to make the first left turn, I told her to assist the dog in making the turn by holding her right hand under the dog's jaw. To help her to remember to use her right hand, I told her to hold her right hand over her head. When she reached the end of the second leg of the triangle, she again raised her right hand, and then assisted the dog in making the turn. In training it is easy to get things wrong, but Sarah kept on practising until she could make every move automatically. She was then ready to go through the whole exercise without raising her right arm.

At the end of the moving patterns, the handler has to return to the judge, either for the dog to be examined, if this has not already been done, or to pose the dog for the final assessment. Each breed has its set pose. In the case of the Rough Collie, the dog should walk into a natural stance, but in order to illustrate the various methods Sarah walks the dog into pose and then positions its legs. First, she reaches over the dog's back, holding the leg just above the elbow, and bringing it underneath the body. The rear legs are then adjusted and positioned according to the breed's requirements. Some breeds should present an overall square picture, others should be slightly pulled out to the rear. Sarah then positions the front legs to appear parallel to the left front leg, with the elbows tucked well under the body. The space between all the legs should be about the same as the width of the dog. The dog should now be ready for the judge's assessment and should be posed in the same manner as in step one.

Regular exhibitors think nothing of taking their dog into the ring, but for the novice, whether they are a junior or an adult, it

Sarah presents the dog to the judge, standing two metres in front of him. She allows the dog to come forward and lets his jaw rest on the palm of her hand.

The first leg of the triangle. When Sarah is about to make the first left turn, she assists the dog by holding her right hand as illustrated in the first exercise. In order that she remembers to use her right hand, she holds her hand over her head. I always shout out 'where is the sky?' and her hand shoots up.

When she reached the end of the second leg of the triangle, I shouted: "where is the sky?' and up comes the right hand to help the dog to turn left and complete the triangle. Sometimes, as in this case, the handler can get a bit tangled up with the dog, but Sarah was soon completing the exercise perfectly.

Sarah returns to try to pose the dog.

Now she has got the dog in the correct position.

Sarah now starts to pose the dog, first by grasping the dog's leg above the elbow and positioning it. She then repeats the procedure with the other front leg.

Sarah puts the rear leg into position.

The front leg is positioned to appear parallel to the left front leg.

The final pose. The dog should now be looking its very best for the judge's final assessment.

can be a nerve-racking experience. There is nothing you can do about feeling nervous, it is something that diminishes with experience. The best thing you can do in the early stages is practise and practise until you are confident that both you and your dog know what you are doing. If you have got things worked out in the familiar surroundings of your home, the chances are that you will perform better in the show ring. Obviously your technique and confidence will improve if you have the opportunity to go to a training school. A useful tip for the novice is to go to some shows and watch experienced junior handlers in action. You can learn a lot from other people: you can copy their good points and learn from any mistakes they might make.

The essence of being a proficient dog-handler is to be well co-ordinated in your actions and to be gifted with a keen sense of rhythm and balance. You also need to have a fairly extrovert personality that thrives on competition. It is always said that there is no such thing as a perfect dog. Equally, no handler can hope to be perfect. Co-ordination is a natural gift and a handler will struggle to get good results without it. A natural sense of balance and rhythm can be helped by taking ballet lessons, and I would encourage youngsters to improve their natural skills in this way. Basic gymnastics would be of equal value.

One of the best training grounds for young exhibitors is to compete in an Exemption Show. This is a show where the organisers have obtained a licence from the Kennel Club to hold a dog show in aid of a good cause, usually for a rescue scheme or a charity, and it is exempt from Kennel Club rules. Four pedigree classes are classified, with as many novelty classes as the organisers wish to put on.

For the inexperienced junior handler it is an ideal opportunity to get used to being in a show ring. The atmosphere is easy-going and friendly, and you can go through your paces without feeling under too much pressure. If you make a mistake you can correct it without feeling you are being penalised too harshly. It also gives you the chance to give an inexperienced show dog some more training. Puppies under six months old, which are excluded from other shows, are allowed to enter and so they can get used to the large crowds and excitement of the show ring. The small entry fee that is charged is well worth paying in terms of the benefit you and your dog will gain from the experience.

Another option is to attend training classes before getting involved in serious competition. There are a number of Ring Craft clubs, spread throughout the country, and many are now holding special classes for youngsters. I was particularly impressed with the one run by Dorothy Bridges at Longlevens, Gloucestershire, where I was invited to give a seminar for junior handlers.

The classes at this club are organised on a weekly basis, and they are usually attended by about sixteen juniors in ages ranging from three years old to eighteen. On their first visit, the juniors are introduced to each other and to all the dogs. They are given a talk on how to walk and stand their dogs, and are then told to stand behind the more experienced juniors and they try to copy their movements. After about three weeks instruction they are taught to do the more difficult exercises such as the reverse triangle, the figure eight and the letter T. They are also taught about the anatomy of a dog. Show ring etiquette is also covered, and so by the end of about three months the juniors will be confident and competent to show their dogs in smaller shows. The junior handling classes are judged in exactly the same way as at the other shows. The age groups are divided into a class for six to eleven year olds and another class for twelve to sixteen year olds.There is a judge and a steward, and handlers have to go through the same procedures. The difference is that this is a totally informal situation and both judge and steward will make light of any mistakes that are made. I think it is important for the officials to be relaxed in their attitude and offer plenty of encouragement and support to the youngsters so that it is an enjoyable occasion for everyone.

I remember judging at an Exemption Show and a girl, who was six years old, came into the ring with her Cocker Spaniel. She had obviously been watching her mother very closely and she copied her movements exactly, as I noticed when I judged the adult class. The little girl had chosen exactly the right size of dog and she knew what she had to do. The dog had obviously been taught to pose, but it kept moving about and refusing to stand still. Ignoring all the laughter from onlookers, she kept on telling her dog to stand still, and I admired her patience and perseverance as she persisted in trying to pose this lively dog. When I asked her to do the triangle, she set off at full tilt and her legs were going a mile a minute in order to keep up. But she was determined to complete all the procedures and I was convinced that she had the makings of a good handler.

On another occasion I was judging a seven-year-old boy, who was struggling to control a Golden Retriever. He stood in front of me while I examined his dog and then I asked him to move his dog in a straight line away from me towards the other side of the ring. I said: "Do you understand?" He answered: "Yeah." I then said: "Bring the dog back to me and pose it. Do you understand?" Again he replied: "Yeah." Then, on his return when I asked him to pose the dog, he looked completely blank and said: "What's that?" I discovered that this was his third time in a show ring, yet he had not picked up the basics of show ring phraseology. He had also failed to learn that good manners are important, for although you are not being judged for them, a rude or off-hand manner can alienate the judge. There are also certain dos and don'ts which you should master before going into more formal competition. I was judging a young boy at an Exemption Show, and I complimented him on how well he was handling his dog. He said: "I got a first last week." I immediately explained to him that you must never tell the judge about any previous wins. At an Exemption Show, mistakes in handling and in what a youngster says or does, can be excused. But at higher levels these faults would be penalised.

The judge can also learn some useful lessons when it comes to dealing with inexperienced handlers. I recall judging one boy in a six to eleven year old class at St Albans. He was clearly very nervous, but I had been impressed by his handling capabilities. When I was choosing my final winners I said to him: "I am not placing you, but I will have you out." I then walked along the line, picking out those that I wanted to stay. When I came to pick my winners from the final line-up, the boy was not among them. He had left the ring and was standing tearfully by his mother. I went over to him and explained what I had meant. I had not wanted him out of the show ring, I had wanted him out to join the other winners in the centre of the ring. I have never used the expression "I will have have you out" since then.

Above all, the youngster must be keen on competing in junior handling classes. I know of too many parents who are regular showgoers and have pushed their children into the classes, without caring whether the child wanted to join in. On one memorable occasion a small boy was dragged into the ring by a large dog, literally being pushed from behind by his parents. Confused and unhappy, he burst into tears, and it was a great relief when his dog pulled him out of the ring, and I saw no more of either of them.

Competitors line up at the 1989 Windsor Championship Show.

Dalton.

The judge was Lena Ekbom, 1989 International Junior Handler of the Year, pictured with her winner at Windsor.

Dalton

Chapter Three

INTO THE BIG TIME

The level of competition at Open Shows is much higher than at Exemption Shows. They are open to all breeds, with four or five classes for each breed. Junior Handling classes can be held when the organisers have paid a nominal fee for the diploma issued by the Junior Handling Association. This also qualifies those that are placed in the first three of the six to eleven year old class and the first three in the twelve to sixteen-year-old class for a chance to compete in the semi-finals of the Junior Handler of the Year competition, which is held at the Richmond Championship Show. Juniors do not have to be a member of the Junior Handling Association to compete at Open Show level, but if they progress to the semi-finals, they must enrol as members. Richmond is an outdoor show held in September; the classes are usually conducted in the main ring during the lunch break.

The entry at an all-breed Open Show tends to be much larger, as juniors can compete with any breed from the Hounds, Utility, Toy, Working, Gundog and Terrier groups. It is therefore much harder to get in the placings in this type of competition than when a breed club puts on junior handling classes and there is only one breed for the children to handle. The standard of handling will probably be equally high in both types of show. By this stage, you have lost the youngsters who are just competing for a fun day out, and a number will also have dropped out because they have decided that handling in the ring is not for them. The junior handlers in Open Shows are usually very serious about the competition and determined to get through to the Richmond semi-finals. But I have found that juniors are nearly always good sportsmen and get on well with each other in the ring. The pressure mounts, however, when they are surrounded by an audience of parents and critical adults.

Championship Shows are now scheduling Junior Handling classes with increasing regularity. The Champ shows are one stage higher up than Open Shows: Challenge Certificates are awarded and dogs can qualify for Crufts. The junior handling classes are usually held in a ring alongside the breed classes, and everyone involved in the competition prefers this to being put on as a sort of lunch-time entertainment. The entry fee is paid on the day and dogs must be entered in the breed classes by their owners.

Again, a first, second or third placing at a Championship Show qualifies for a place in the Richmond semi-finals, providing the junior becomes a fully paid up member of the Junior Handling Association. Now that junior handling has increased so much in popularity, entries are often large and the standard is getting higher all the time. The juniors deserve to be judged by those that are suitably qualified. Judges need to be objective, ignoring the quality of the dog and concentrating exclusively on the individual's ability to control the dog in the ring.

At this level of competition, the dog being handled by a junior will also be competing with the top dogs in the breed class. It can therefore be assumed that the dog is in good show condition. Juniors are not being judged specifically on the appearance of the dog, but a well turned out entry is obviously a bonus as it will attract the judge's attention. Hopefully, juniors will have helped their parents with the pre-show preparation – the bathing, trimming and grooming – and assembled everything that is needed for the day of the show.

I would suggest you pack:

1. Benching towel.
2. Benching chain (if your dog is used to being secured with this, rather than an ordinary lead).
3. Show collar and lead or a choke chain, plus a spare set of all these items in case of emergency.
4. Drinking bowl.
5. Drinking water – this saves you having to walk miles to find the nearest tap.
6. Water sprayer (the type that is used on house plants).
7. Shampoo.
8 Brush and comb.
9. Scissors.
10. Throat spray (this is for medicinal purposes, as on a hot day a dog's throat can easily get sore when it is on a choke chain or being fed with dry titbits).

When you get to the show ring, you will find there is no set procedure for the junior handling class. Some organisers will give you separate ring numbers, others use the ones allocated for the breed classes. It is an area that could be improved, as it can be confusing trying to work out where you should be at a specific time if you are at a large show. Before the junior handling class, the dog can be given a few last-minute preparations.

Before it goes into the breed class, it will have been given a final grooming, and on long-coated breeds any untidy hair, such as that which grows between the toes or on the hocks, will have been trimmed. It is a good idea to check that the dog's feet have not got dirty en route to the ring. Obviously the smaller breeds can be carried, but on a wet day the larger breeds can get mud-spattered. That is where the water sprayer and the dry shampoo come in handy. I usually use Vetzyme foam shampoo or Ring 5 quick clean self-rinsing shampoo, which help to clean the white hairs on my dogs. Again, I stress that the judge is not marking you on the dog's individual appearance, but if you are going to compete, you may as well make sure you have everything right. When you go to the ring, make sure you bring a brush or comb, if you have a long-coated dog.

Some handlers of smooth-coated breeds, such as the Rottweiler, bring a leather to the ringside, in order to give the dog a final polish. All handlers need to bring a spare show collar and lead to the ring, plus any titbit, if the dog is to be baited.

The milestone for every ambitious junior handler is to reach the Richmond semi-finals. This is held at the Royal Ascot Racecourse in September and is part of the Richmond Championship Show. The whole junior handling competition is organised by Liz Cartledge, and youngsters are given a gift to commemorate the day, a luncheon pass, and a ring number, and are told which ring they will be judged in. The only drawback is that the rings that are allocated for the junior handlers have to be vacated by a certain time for the breed judging to commence. The junior handling competition is now such an important event that it is time that it was organised as a separate competition on its own, or run in conjunction with the Kennel Club Junior Organisation, which caters for obedience and agility events for juniors. At the Richmond semi-finals, there are now about five hundred handlers competing to go through to the final to find the Junior Handler of the Year. The entries are judged in the six groups – Toy, Utility, Gundogs, Terriers, Working and Hounds – and these are divided into the two age-groups, six to eleven and twelve to sixteen. The winner in each class goes through to the final, and so there are two representatives from each group who qualify, making a total of twelve entries for the final, which is held the following January, usually at the Hotel Metropole in Birmingham.

Chapter Four

IT'S TOUGH AT THE TOP

It is when you reach the final of the Junior Handler of the Year that the format of the competition changes. At all levels from Exemption Show up to the Richmond semi-finals, you are required to go through the set exercises with your chosen dog. At the final, and later at the International Final, you are required to change dogs. I think, at the moment, I am the only judge who asks juniors to change dogs at Open Show and Championship Show level. I usually choose a couple of well-behaved dogs, and then the juniors in my final line-up will be asked to move the dog that is unfamiliar to them. This is not a mandatory part of the competition, it is left to the judge's discretion. The reason I do it is because it shows me if a handler can change his style to suit the dog. This is particularly revealing when the juniors are having to perform under pressure.

At the final of the Junior Handler of the Year there are twelve competitors, two from each group. They are drawn equally from the two age-groups, but at this final stage, all ages compete against each other. The juniors are asked to go through the set exercises – presenting the dog for the judge's inspection, and

Simon Briggs (centre) from Australia was the winner of the 1987 International Final.

Derek Whitehouse

Clint Livingstone (centre) from the USA was the 1988 International Junior handler of the Year.

Derek Whitehouse

then moving – with their chosen dog. Then they leave the ring and must return with a different breed and go through the routine again. The organisers try to make sure that the juniors are given a completely different breed, so they go from a large dog to a small dog, or vice versa. The object of the exercise is to see if the junior is capable of controlling a strange dog, and can adapt his style of handling to suit that particular breed. The winner is given the title Junior Handler of the Year and goes through to compete in the International Final at Crufts.

The International Final is now becoming a major highlight of Crufts, and in 1990 there were eighteen countries taking part. The latest recruits were Malta, Portugal, Canada and Monaco. Because of the British quarantine laws, all the competitors must select British-based dogs. In order to be totally fair, this also includes the UK representative. Thanks to the good will of the top breeders, the juniors can virtually choose any breed they like. But they will only have a chance to practise with the dog on the day of the competition, perhaps two hours before judging starts. Obviously, the juniors have no responsibility for the physical appearance of the dog, but as they are competing at the world's most famous dog show, the quality of dogs and the standard of presentation is extremely high.

The juniors have to go through the set exercises with the dog of their choice, and then they leave the ring. They then return with a different dog. Again, Liz Cartledge of the Junior Handling Association works hard to ensure that there is a good contrast in the two breeds the junior has to handle. At this level of competition, the judge will be looking closely at how the junior gaits with the two different breeds. He will be watching to see if they can keep pace with the big-striding breeds, such as the German Shepherd Dog and the Dobermann Pinscher, and then alter their pace to suit a light-stepping toy dog like the Papillon. When the judge is examining the dog, he will be watching to see if the junior is firm and authoritative with the big breeds, and then can be delicate and graceful when handling a small dog. After the second set of exercises has been completed, all the juniors return to the ring with their first choice of dog, and then the judge will make his final assessment.

The standard of competition is becoming higher every year,

and all the judges I have spoken to, who have had the honour of adjudicating the International Final, have had their work cut out to find their winner. I judged the 1989 International Final, and I was very impressed with a number of the juniors. Stephanie Godfrey from Australia chose an Irish Setter as her first choice, and then changed to a Pekingese. She handled both very competently, as you would expect from someone who had reached the final three years previously. Tony Portelli was representing Malta, and this was the first time his country had taken part in the competition. He placed his American Cocker Spaniel on the table for my inspection, and apart from a slight awkwardness in the placing of his dog, he conducted himself very professionally. It was in the second round that things started to go wrong. He was given an Afghan Hound, who proved very reluctant to move. Tony persisted, trying to encourage the dog, but it still resisted his advances. He was holding a brush in his hand, and I wondered if this was making the dog nervous, so I took it from him. Then, with marvellous patience, he eventually encouraged the dog to move in a triangle. I think this proved an important point: things can go wrong, no matter how professional you are. But if you keep calm, and show patience and sympathy, you will win over the dog – and the judge. Bad luck stayed with him in the final round when his American Cocker Spaniel slipped its lead, and came over toward me. But even with all these mishaps, Tony's style of handling stood out and I selected him in my final six.

Tina Kening from Canada impressed me with the way she handled a Shetland Sheepdog. She was very workmanlike in her approach, and the dog responded well. In the second round she handled a lively Standard Poodle, and again did very well. At the final stage, she had a momentary lapse in concentration, but she recovered well, regained her composure and carried on like a professional. You always have to remember the pressure on juniors competing at this level of competition – all of them on strange territory, some having to cope with a foreign language. In fact, my knowledge of Spanish came in useful with Marita Rufino from Portugal and Jose Haro Kay, an eleven-year-old from Spain. My eventual winner was Lena Ekbom from Sweden. She was aged fifteen at the time of the competition and she had

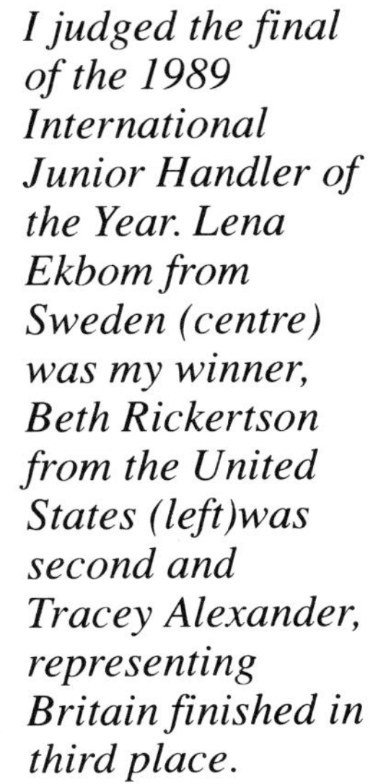

I judged the final of the 1989 International Junior Handler of the Year. Lena Ekbom from Sweden (centre) was my winner, Beth Rickertson from the United States (left)was second and Tracey Alexander, representing Britain finished in third place.

Derek Whitehouse

Competitors for the 1990 International Final. The winner, Pernilla Wistead from Sweden, is in the front row with the Shih Tzu she handled.

Derek Whitehouse

Carl Johnson judged the 1990 International Final.

been handling West Highland White Terriers since she was eight years old. She handled a Westie in the first round, and I was very impressed by her style and confidence. This increased when she was asked to move the dog. In the second round she had a Saluki, and again, she was calm, confident and stylish. I was almost splitting hairs to find a winner, and it was this calm confident manner under pressure that swayed my decision.

Beth Rickertson from the United States came second. It suited her well to handle a dainty Pomeranian, and her control of the Saluki appeared effortless. Tracey Alexander, under terrific pressure as the UK representative, handled a Bichon Frise and then an English Pointer, and she finished third. Her whole approach was professional and she was smartly and suitably dressed in a black skirt and a red blazer. It was a great day for me, and for all the competitors, and I felt that junior handling was truly becoming a force to be reckoned with.

In 1990 Carl Johnson was invited to judge the international Final. He is well known as a handler, campaigning his wife's famous Dicarl Great Danes. He has won the Working Group at Crufts, and is also a successful handler of Schnauzers and King Charles Spaniels. He has taken an interest in junior handling for a number of years, and he was impressed by the high standard of the competitors in the international line-up. Suzie Roffey, representing Britain came third, giving a competent and confident performance. Andrew Boatwright from the USA was runner-up.

"Andrew had all the attributes of a terrier handler," said Carl in his write-up of the competition. "He had obviously spent a great deal of time with some great terrier men. Cool, nothing fazed him, he gave a professional performance."

But again, honours went to Sweden with Pernilla Wistead becoming the International Junior Handler of the Year.

"At fourteen years old, this young handler impressed me from the minute she entered the ring," said Carl. "Never for one moment did her concentration waver. She had what I was looking for, complete control of her charge, both the Shih Tzu and the changeover dog. She is a natural, her use of the lead was exceptional and she has that almost indefinable something that makes a star. In dogs we may call it ring presence.

"Pernilla was a worthy winner of seventeen worthy qualifiers. All were winners in this final, there were no losers, I just had the honour and pleasure of placing seventeen winners."

Chapter Five

DRESS SENSE

Choosing the right clothes for the occasion is very important, not because you are being judged on your personal appearance but because the wrong sort of clothes can detract from what you are trying to do. The judge wants to concentrate all his attention on the way you handle the dog; he does not want to be distracted by fussy frills or put off by a shoddy down-at-heel appearance. Equally, you want to feel comfortable so you can concentrate on your dog without worrying about what you look like.

Shoes are probably the most important item, as you will need to gait with your dog without fear of slipping on wet grass if you are outside, or on slippery wood or tile floors if you are handling inside. I personally do not like to see youngsters wearing plimsolls, comfortable as they are. But a smart pair of trainers are perfectly acceptable, if they are worn with the appropriate clothes. Girls should never wear shoes with high heels. Not only are these dangerous for the handler, but it could be very painful if a dog's foot was stepped on.

In the early days before junior handling became a serious competition, the temptation was for doting parents to dress up small children to look cute. This is not the object of the exercise. Youngsters should think in terms of choosing a sensible working outfit. Avoid loud colours and anything that is too outlandish. The ideal is smart trousers with a shirt or jumper and a jacket or body-warmer. Girls can obviously wear dresses, as long as they are of a sensible length. Girls who are handling small dogs should not wear long flared skirts as the dog gets tangled in the skirt or is hidden from the judge's view. Some choose to dress in the same colour as the dog they will be handling, and this can look attractive and eye-catching without being too flamboyant.

Johanna Vos, representing New Zealand in the International Final at Crufts is smart, but sensibly dressed.

Remember, you cannot rely on the weather if you are competing outside, so you should always come prepared with a raincoat and Wellington boots. There is nothing wrong with having a look at other exhibitors and taking note of how they dress. I have noticed a couple of handlers who have tried to emulate Marita Gibbs both in handling style and in the manner in which she dresses. That is a smart thing to do, as Marita excels in both these areas. Girls with long hair should wear it tied back. I remember watching a video of a girl being judged in a handling class, and she had long blonde hair which was being blown about in the wind. She spent most of her time pushing it away from her face, and she was obviously finding it hard to concentrate fully

Dryston Furby is dressed for an outside show. He looks neat and comfortable.

on her dog. It is easier for boys to dress for the occasion as their choice is more limited. If a jacket is worn, it should be buttoned, and a tie should be secured by a tie pin to prevent it flapping. I do not consider either a jacket or tie to be essential. The most important thing is to look clean and smart, and to feel comfortable. When I exhibit in breed classes I usually wear neatly pressed trousers and a jumper or body-warmer. But when I am judging or stewarding I wear a suit and a tie. I think it is important to look the part and to set a good example. Remember, it is not a fashion parade. You are being judged on your ability to handle a dog. You should, however, give yourself every chance of success and not let yourself down with unsuitable attire.

If you are going to carry a brush or comb with you into the ring, you should have a pocket or holder of some kind, so that when you are required to use both hands, you do not have to worry about where you are going to put the accessories. Some handlers just leave their brush or comb on the ground, but then when you have finished your exercise, you have all the bother of coming back to retrieve it. If you are accustomed to using titbits, these should also be kept in a pocket so that your hands are free and the dog is not constantly looking for the snack. Titbits have their uses, particularly when you need to encourage a dog that is unsure of itself, or if you have to handle a strange dog.

The dogs that junior handlers bring into the ring must be clean and well groomed and free from offensive odours. There is nothing worse for a judge than having to examine a dirty dog. Personally, I want to examine all the dogs in the class and finish up still looking clean and smart, and not smelling as if I have just cleaned the kennels. The final consideration is the type of collar, chain or lead you are going to use in the ring. To a large extent this depends on the breed of dog that is being handled, but every handler has his own preference. I have always used a thin but strong check-chain attached to a leather lead, about one centimetre thick. The leather is very pliable, so I can manipulate it easily with one hand. I always remove the snap fastening as I think it makes the lead much lighter and it is easier to control the dog without having the metal snap dangling in the way. Most of the dogs that I handle are from 45 to 70 centimetres at the shoulder. But I have also handled Shetland Sheepdogs and Miniature Poodles with the same type of chain and lead, though lighter in weight. Some handlers prefer not to use a chain, as some dogs will pull away and then gag and buck at the feel of a check-chain around their neck. If the dog you are exhibiting is small and biddable, a light slip-lead can be used. This is usually made of nylon with an adjustable loop at the end to be slipped over the dog's head. Other handlers use a lead that is half chain used with a part nylon collar. With the larger breeds I think you need a strong leather collar and lead, as this will give the handler more control over the dog.

Chapter Six

CHOOSING YOUR DOG

The choice of dog you handle is very often influenced by the dogs you have at home. Many parents who show dogs regularly are delighted that their child is taking an interest in their hobby or business, and are only too pleased to allocate one of the family dogs. There are a few exceptions: for instance, parents who are reluctant to have their prize-winning dog exposed to any incident that might occur in the junior handling ring. But most are keen to support and encourage junior handlers.

It is definitely an advantage if you are used to going to shows regularly and you can look at the professional handlers in different breed rings, and get an idea of what style of handling is required. If you compete at the top level, you will need to change dogs, and therefore the more you can assimilate about handling different breeds, the easier you will find it. When you have watched a variety of different handlers, it will also help you to decide what you want to incorporate into your own system of handling. If you decide to go for a different breed than the one you have at home, you will still find it useful to practise at home. The more practice you get, the better your overall performance will be. Sometimes an individual's style of handling is simply not suited to a particular breed of dog. I judged one junior with a Great Dane a few years ago, and although she was good enough to keep in my final seven, she did not make the final line-up. I told her that some judges might approve of her style of handling, but I preferred less action and more precise handling. It seemed that all her efforts were spent on trying to stop the dog from shying away, and her style was wasted in trying to make her dog move properly. There appeared to be no rapport between the two of them. I felt that she had chosen the wrong dog, and I suggested that she might do better with an Afghan, a German Shepherd or a Dobermann. She was naturally quick and light on her feet, and this would complement the way these breeds moved. I judged her again about two years later, and she still had the same dog. I was pleased to see that she had worked very hard with the dog: it had gained in confidence and stood calmly for inspection. But that did not alter my opinion that she was capable of excelling if she had a different breed of dog. The last time I saw her, she was handling a Dobermann, and she walked away the winner of her class. She always had the capabilities – she just needed the right dog for them to shine out.

All breeds need to be handled differently, and temperament is as important a consideration as size. It is the handler, not the dog that is under scrutiny, but if there is a strong partnership between dog and handler working in harmony, it will certainly attract the judge's attention. At Exemption Shows the crowds love to see a small child attempting to control an unruly puppy, and some judges will actually choose someone like this as their winner. But they are just playing to the audience, and the serious-minded youngsters who have handled their dogs well and done everything right, have a right to wonder what went wrong. Even if you are only competing in an Exemption Show, you should be judged according to ability, for this is the training ground for junior handlers of the future.

The dog you choose will either help you to win or hold you back from winning, so a lot of thought should go into the choice you make. A badly behaved dog will waste the judge's time and probably upset the other dogs in the ring. On the other hand, a good representative of a breed will draw attention to the handler, especially if it is clean with a gleaming well-groomed coat. The dog does not have to be a top winner in its own right; it is temperament, patience and co-operation that is more important. The dog's reputation will not be damaged if you are not placed; equally it is not the dog's fault if it has obeyed all your commands and you are not placed. Always praise your dog, no matter the result. The competition should be an enjoyable experience for both you and your dog. There is always something new to learn, and you will probably do better next time.

When you are choosing a dog to handle, it is sometimes best to consider how easy it will be to control the dog in the ring, rather than going for your personal favourite, regardless of temperament. There are some juniors that really excel at making a St. Bernard or a Newfoundland look good – both standing and on the move. I once judged a young girl of medium height, handling a St. Bernard, and she made it look very easy. She also handled a small dog with the same amount of determination, yet she was gentle and caring in her manner towards the dog. At another show, I judged a young boy, who handled a Staffordshire Bull Terrier extremely well. He was obviously trying to present a rather macho image, although he was neatly dressed and well-mannered. He was kneeling beside his dog, yet I could still view it from all sides, as he had placed it with its front towards me, as seen in the breed ring. He moved the dog with a nice brisk pace, keeping the lead taut only when needed. He then stopped about two metres in front of me, and posed the dog as if to say: "There he is, look at him!" I was very impressed with his manner of handling, but when I asked him to handle a West Highland White Terrier, he was unable to change his style of handing. The dog in question had a sound temperament, but it almost visibly crumbled; it could not cope with the boy's domineering character.

If you choose a long-coated breed, you will probably want to take a brush into the ring, to give the dog a final tidy-up. This should be kept in a pocket or tucked into a belt, so that it does not get in the way. There is nothing wrong with giving the dog a final brush-up, but it is something else to do, and you may find it easier to handle a dog that does not need this extra attention. Some breeds are expected to show a keen and alert expression, and some handlers use titbits to achieve this, baiting the dog to pose with ears tipped or pricked. But the use of titbits can also cause problems if the dog is constantly ferreting around for the reward. On the other hand, they can help to keep an unruly dog interested in its handler. It is difficult to weigh up the pros and cons; it comes down to a personal choice and will largely depend on whether the dog has been trained to expect a reward.

Some breeds, like those in the Terrier Group, are usually shown on a tight lead, and they respond well to that method. But breeds like the Border Collie and Bearded Collie, the Shetland Sheepdog and most of the Toy Group, some of the Hound Group and many of the Utility Group, move much better when shown on a loose lead. You must study the breed you have chosen to see how it gaits, and then ensure that it is trained to accept a loose lead if it has a smooth, flowing and far-reaching gait, or the tight lead for the Terrier Group.

The Otterhound has a unique loose and shambling walk, but as it steps up in pace it breaks into a long-striding, sound, active trot. Any breed standard that describes the gait as "Easy and Active" should be shown on a loose lead; this includes the Irish Wolfhound and the Deerhound. The Whippet's movement is described as: "Free, hind-legs coming well under the body for propulsion, forelegs thrown well forward low over the ground, true coming and going." The only way a Whippet can show that sort of movement is on a loose lead, not strung up. If you choose an Afghan, the standard suggests that the gait should be: "Smooth and springy with a style of high order." This is not easy to achieve and only older children should attempt to handle an Afghan. Gundogs on the move look very striking with their far-reaching gait, and again they need the freedom to move on a loose lead.

When it comes to the Toy Group, the standard, in many instances, asks for a breed's gait to be "Free with drive". In the case of the Yorkshire Terrier and the Pom it should be: "Free moving, brisk and buoyant". The Pug is expected to have a slight roll of the hindquarters to typify its gait, and the Italian Greyhound should be "High stepping and have free action".

From this variety of gaits, it is easy to see the importance of choosing the size, shape and type of dog to suit your own size, strength, and personality. I would not suggest that any breed was totally unsuitable for a junior; it all depends on the temperament of the individual dog. A Rottweiler, Dobermann Pinscher or a Japanese Akita – all breeds that have a dominant character – can be handled as impressively by a youngster as the smaller or more submissive breeds, as long as the junior has sufficient authority and control, and the dog is used to co-operating in the show ring.

The breeds registered with the English Kennel Club are divided into the six groups – Hound, Working, Utility, Terrier, Toy and Gundogs. The Working Group is by far the largest with forty-four breeds and there is some pressure for this to be divided into Guarding and Shepherding Groups, but as yet no decision has been reached.

Breeds registered with the English Kennel Club

Hound Group

Afghan Hound
Basenji
Basset Hound
Basset Fauve de Bretagne
Beagle
Bloodhound
Borzoi
Dachshunds: Standard and Miniature (Wire, Long-coated, and Smooth)
Deerhound
Elkhound
Finnish Spitz
Greyhound
Hamiltonstovare
Ibizan Hound
Irish Wolfhound
Otterhound
Petit Basset Griffon Vendeen

Pharaoh Hound
Rhodesian Ridgeback
Saluki
Sloughi
Whippet

Terrier Group

Airedale Terrier
Australian Terrier
Bedlington Terrier
Border Terrier
Bull Terrier and Miniature Bull Terrier
Cairn Terrier
Dandie Dinmont Terrier
Fox Terrier: Wire and Smooth
Glen of Imaal Terrier
Irish Terrier
Kerry Blue Terrier
Lakeland Terrier
Manchester Terrier
Norfolk Terrier
Norwich Terrier
Scottish Terrier
Sealyham Terrier
Skye Terrier
Soft-Coated Wheaten Terrier
Staffordshire Bull Terrier
Welsh Terrier
West Highland White Terrier

Utility Group

Boston Terrier
Bulldog
Chow Chow

French Bulldog
German Spitz
Japanese Akita
Japanese Spitz
Keeshond
Leonberger
Lhaso Apso
Miniature Schnauzer
Poodles: Standard, Miniature and Toy
Schipperke
Schnauzer
Shar Pei
Shih Tzu
Tibetan Spaniel
Tibetan Terrier

Toy Group

Affenpinscher
Australian Silky Terrier
Bichon Frise
Cavalier King Charles Spaniel
Chinese Crested
Chihuahua: Smooth Coat and Long Coat
English Toy Terrier (Black and Tan)
Griffon Bruxellois
Italian Greyhound
Japanese Chin
King Charles Spaniel
Lowchen
Maltese
Miniature Pinscher
Papillon
Pekingese
Pomeranian
Pug
Yorkshire Terrier

Working Group

Alaskan Malamute
Anatolian Shepherd Dog
Australian Cattle Dog
Australian Kelpie
Bearded Collie
Belgian Shepherd Dogs: Groenendael, Laekenois, Malinois, and Tervueren
Bernese Mountain Dog
Border Collie
Bouvier des Flandres
Boxer
Briard
Bullmastiff
Collie Rough and Smooth
Dobermann
Eskimo Dog
Estrela Mountain Dog
German Shepherd Dog (Alsatian)
Giant Schnauzer
Great Dane
Hovawart
Hungarian Puli
Komondor
Lancashire Heeler
Maremma Sheepdog
Mastiff
Neopolitan Mastiff
Newfoundland
Norwegian Buhund
Old English Sheepdog
Pinscher
Polish Lowland Sheepdog
Portuguese Water Dog
Pyrenean Mountain Dog
Rottweiler
St. Bernard
Samoyed

Shetland Sheepdog
Siberian Husky
Swedish Vallhund
Tibetan Mastiff
Welsh Corgi: Pembroke and Cardigan

Gundog Group

Brittany
English Setter
German Shorthaired Pointer
German Wirehaired Pointer
Gordon Setter
Irish Setter
Hungarian Vizsla
Irish Red and White Setter
Italian Spinone
Large Munsterlander
Pointer
Chesapeake Bay Retriever
Curly Coated Retriever
Flat Coated Retriever
Golden Retriever
Labrador Retriever
American Cocker Spaniel
Clumber Spaniel
Cocker Spaniel
English Springer
Field Spaniel
Irish Water Spaniel
Sussex Spaniel
Welsh Springer
Weimaraner: Smooth and Wire

Chapter Seven

TABLE DOGS

The world of handling is divided into 'table dogs' and 'non table dogs' – and this depends on where the dog is posed for examination by the judge. Obviously, the size of the dog is the crucial element, and consequently all members of the Toy Group are table dogs. This procedure is followed mostly for the convenience of the judges, so they do not have to crouch down or kneel on the ground in order to assess the dog. The tinies, such as the Chihuahua, Yorkshire Terrier, Pekingese, Papillon, Maltese and Japanese Chin, take up very little room on the table, and so they can be manipulated into a good pose if they are used to being lifted up and examined on the table at home. The larger and heavier breeds in the Toy Group, such as the Cavalier King Charles Spaniel, King Charles Spaniel, Pug, Australian Silky and English Toy Terrier, take a little more effort for a small handler to lift on to a table and then arrange in a show stance.

There are only two breeds in the Gundog Group that are shown on the table. These are the American Cocker Spaniel and the English Cocker Spaniel. Both are biddable types and seem to settle well into the routine of a table assessment. The Working

Welsh Corgi (Pembroke) Height: 25·4–30·5cms. Excellent dog for a child to show. No tail to worry about and has a super temperament.

Tibetan Spaniel Height: 25·4cms. Happy, friendly dogs. Usually baited.

Miniature Poodle Height: 28-38cms. Requires a lot of setting up, but a lot easier to handle than the Standard Poodle. Looks elegant on a loose lead. The same applies to the Toy Poodle, which is only 28cms in height.

Cavalier King Charles Spaniel Height is not stipulated in the Breed Standard, but the weight should be between 12-16lbs. This is a happy little dog and does not need much handling to show well. It should be stacked on the table and moved with a loose lead. Ideal for the younger age group.

Bedlington Terrier
Height: Approx 66cms.
This dog needs a lot of preparation before the show, but relatively little attention in the ring. This is a dainty dog and requires sensitive handling.

Pearce

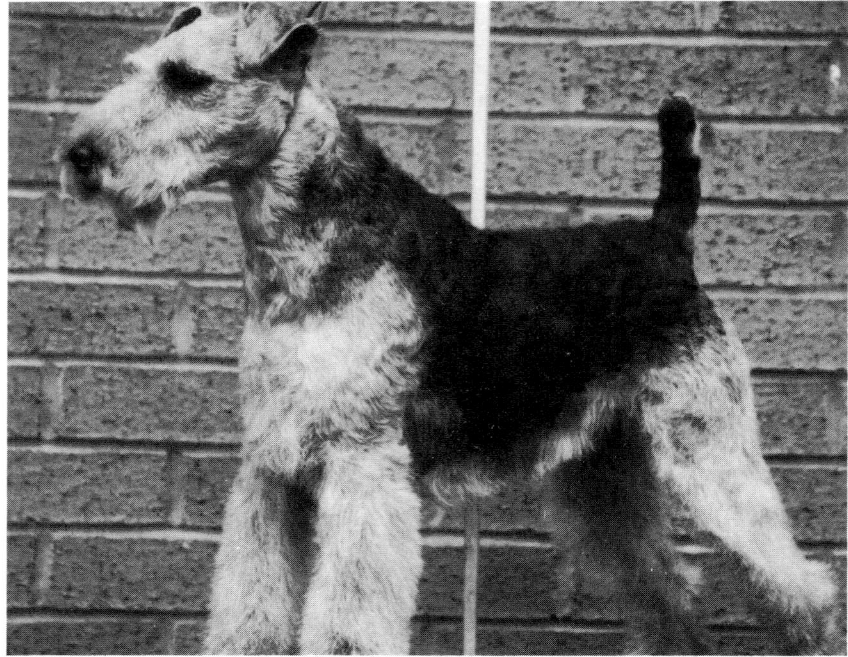

Welsh Terrier
Height: 39cms maximum.
Moved on a tight lead, terrier-style. Ideal for juniors as it looks smart with a minimum of handling.

Shetland Sheepdog
Height: dogs 37cms, bitches 35·5cms.
Stacked on the table, needs tidying up in the ring. Easy to handle, ideal for juniors.

Beagle
Height: 33-40cms
Stacked on the table, the tail needs to be supported. It should not need to be baited. Usually shown on a tight lead.

Cooke

French Bulldog Height: Related to the weight – dogs 28lbs, bitches 24lbs. This is the only bulldog shown on the table. It is stacked and shown on a loose lead. It has a slow gait and a sweet temper.

Staffordshire Bull Terrier Height: Related to the weight – dogs 28-38lbs, bitches 24-34lbs. Shown facing the judge. Despite its small size (approx 35cms), this is a breed that needs firm handling for it is surprisingly strong.

Dalton

West Highland White Terrier Height: 28cms. Stacked on the table with the tail held up. Ideal for juniors. Moved on a tight lead.

Smooth Fox Terrier Weight: dogs 16-18lbs, bitches 15-17lbs. Active little dog which moves quickly and smartly.

Group is the largest in terms of numbers, and there are six breeds that are shown on the table. The two types of Welsh Corgi – the Cardigan and the Pembroke – need a table assessment because of their short legs. The Shetland Sheepdog with its profuse coat, needs to be handled so that the judge can feel the body under the coat, the depth of brisket and rib-cage and the tail set. The Swedish Vallhund, the Norwegian Buhund and the Lancashire Heeler are all small in size and need to be examined on the table.

In the Hound Group, the Whippet, which stands at 47cms, is supposed to stand over a lot of ground, so it should not be posed to look square on the table. If the table is narrow, it is best to stand the dog lengthwise. Some handlers with small breeds leave the dog's lead on the table, allowing the dog to stand on its own. I always like to see a loose lead, but I think the handler should always hold on to the end of the lead to ensure the dog is secure and not likely to hurt itself by suddenly jumping off. The Whippet differs again because it looks more elegant if the lead is tucked up in the palm of the hand and held just behind the dog's ears, making the neck look long and arched. The Beagle is also shown on the table, and this was the first small dog I handled in the show ring. I must admit I found it a very strange experience and I felt awkward about posing the dog. But it is all a matter of adapting to the different requirements of each breed. The Basenji and all the six types of Dachshund complete the line-up of table dogs in the Hound Group.

In the Terrier Group, the Wire and Smooth Fox Terriers should be posed on a table with the slip lead held in the palm of the hand, and held just above the neck to emphasise the arch of the neck. The other hand should be used to support the docked tail in the correct position – this also applies to the Scottish Terrier, the West Highland White Terrier and the Irish, Lakeland and Welsh Terriers. The Bedlington Terrier, with its low-set tail needs no such assistance, and in common with the other breeds in the group, the terrier's out-going temperament means that it usually holds its tail in the correct position.

The French Bulldog, a member of the Utility Group, needs to be shown on a table, but this does not apply to the English Bulldog, which is judged standing foursquare on the ground, like the Staffordshire Bull Terrier. The German and Japanese Spitz, the Lhaso Apso, the Shih Tzu, the Tibetan Spaniel and the Schipperke are small enough for table assessment. The Toy and Miniature Poodle are also table dogs, but the Standard Poodle is, of course, judged on the ground.

Before you place your dog on the table, glance at the ring steward for a sign that you should proceed. When you are given the okay, go to the far side of the table, away from the judge, and place your dog facing either left-to-right or right-to-left, as long as it is facing the edge of the table. The judge should be able to examine the dog without having to reach halfway across the table. Do not present the rear of the dog until the judge is ready to examine tail set and rear angulation, and only then, if the judge specifically asks you to position the dog in this way. When the judge stands back to view the dog from the side, the handler should pose it to emphasise its good points as much as possible. The judge will then move round to the front, and the handler must move to the side, all the time holding the dog steady by the lead or collar. When the judge asks to see the dog's teeth, you must assist him without getting in his way. I have noticed that many exhibitors bend over to look at the teeth as well, and this is no help to anyone. The judge will choose which side he wants to look at for his final assessment, and the handler must move out of the way, while still holding the lead.

Sometimes it is necessary for the handler to pass between the dog and the judge. This is far from ideal, but if this happens, try to move as quickly and gracefully as possible and it will be forgiven, especially if the table is long and awkwardly situated so the handler would have to scramble to get back to the other side. If you are tall and handling a small dog, you must make sure you do not crowd the dog. Stand back from the table so that the judge has free access. If you are small, it can be difficult to lift a dog on to the table, especially if you are also carrying a brush or a titbit. That is why you should help yourself by making sure you have a pocket for these extras. Then, at least, you can be sure of having both hands free at all times to control the dog. After the judge's examination on the table, you will be asked to move your dog, and then stand back in line. This gives the judge a last-minute chance to look at your dog, alongside the other competitors. It is best to kneel at the side of your dog, in order to get it into its show pose. I have agreed to judge a table dog on the ground on a number of occasions. This has usually been when a handler's size makes it very difficult for them to lift the dog on to the table. If you ask politely, there are very few judges who would make any objections.

I always used to consider that small dogs were the easiest to control and handle, but I have now come to the conclusion that I was watching outstanding handlers with years of experience behind them. These dogs have a hearty, yet dainty temperament, with a definite character of their own. Many of the tinies appear to have no fear of the bigger dogs, and when I have been in the ring with a large dog, I have often been amused to see one barking and growling at my dog. But I have never minded one jot, for the big dog looks at the tiny one with such interest, ears pricked, and in a stance that I could not produce, no matter how hard I tried!

Chapter Eight

NON TABLE DOGS

The larger breeds of dog are usually posed for inspection near the judge's table or in the centre of the ring. The handler should pose the dog a distance of at least two metres away from the judge, presenting either the left or right side of the dog. The exception to this rule is if you are exhibiting a dog from one of the Bull breeds, such as a Staffordshire Bull Terrier or an English Bulldog, and then the customary procedure is to set the dog up so the judge can view it from the front. The handler should stand beside the dog, opposite to the side where the judge is viewing. There is no need to move as the judge approaches to inspect the dog's front assembly, head and teeth. Some handlers prefer to stand directly in front of the dog, attracting its attention by baiting it, so that the dog stands still and the judge can see it in profile. If you choose this method, you must step to the side as the judge approaches to view the dog's front, so that you are not standing in the way. Again, when the judge is inspecting the dog's teeth, make sure he has plenty of room to manoeuvre. The judge will continue on his way round the dog to view the rear, and the handler should move round to the dog's head to hold it

German Shepherd Dog Height: dogs 57-60cms, bitches 56-57cms. Ideal for the 12-16 age group. Gaited at a good pace, no baiting is required. Sound temperament.

Pearce

Border Collie Height: dogs 53cms, bitches slightly less. A natural, working dog, so handling should be as free as possible. It should be walked into a natural pose, and moved at a brisk pace. It can be baited to give an alert expression, but it is so intelligent, this should not be necessary.
Marc Henrie

Boxer
Height: dogs 57-63cms, bitches 53-59cms. Usually stacked, and baited as it needs to show an alert expression. A tight lead is needed for this strong macho dog.

Samoyed
Height: dogs 51-56cms, bitches 46-51cms.
Always baited, requires firm handling. Happy temperament, shown on a loose lead.

Keeshond
Height: dogs: 45·7cms, bitches 42·3cms. Shown in a similar style to the Samoyed and the Norwegian Buhund. Usually baited, and walked into a natural pose.

Smooth Collie Height: dogs 56-61cms, bitches 51-56cms. Very placid temperament, should be moved at a brisk pace. Usually baited to get an eager expression, with semi-erect ears.

Standard Poodle
Height: Over 38cms
This breed can look very impressive in the right hands. A lively dog that needs a lot of training.

St Bernard
Height: The taller the better, as long as the substance and proportions are maintained. Only the most ambitious junior should attempt to handle this breed. I have seen grown men struggle with it.

Japanese Akita
Height: dogs 66-71cms, bitches 61-66cms.
This breed has to be fully understood to get the best from it. It looks very impressive in the right hands, but it requires firm handling. It should be gaited at a brisk pace.

Bearded Collie Height: dogs 53-56cms, bitches 51-53cms. Free-flowing movement, should be shown on a loose lead and walked into a natural pose.

Golden Retriever Height: dogs 56-61cms, bitches 51-56cms. The tail needs to be held out to show the featherings. Shown on a loose lead, nice easy-going temperament.

Old English Sheepdog Height: dogs 61cms, bitches 56cms. Stands full-square, and should be moved at a brisk pace. Requires a lot of grooming before the show, and a brush and comb needs to be taken into the ring.

Saluki
Height: 58·4-71cms, bitches smaller.
Needs to be encouraged with gentle handling. Moves very gracefully on a loose lead. This breed is not usually baited.

Siberian Husky Height: dogs 53-60cms, bitches 51-56cms. Active type, moves at a good pace. Usually baited and shown on a loose lead.

Bouvier Des Flandres
Height: dogs 62-68cms, bitches 59-65cms.
This breed is a handful for a small child to handle. It should be walked into a natural pose and shown on a loose lead. It should not require baiting or grooming in the ring.

Rottweiler
Height: dogs 63-69cms, bitches 58-63·5cms.
A powerful dog that requires strong, firm handling. The handler needs to be on the alert at all times in the show ring.

Pearce

Bernese Mountain Dog Height: dogs 64-70cms, bitches 58-66cms. Always stacked on the ground. Moved at a brisk pace. Nice, steady temperament.

Komondor
Height: dogs 65-80cms, bitches 55-70cms. Classed as a rare breed, this is a strong-willed dog that takes a lot of handling. The coat is corded, and so it needs preparation for the show ring.

steady. The judge might then stand back and view the dog again, before asking the handler to move it.

The very large dogs in the Working Group, such as the St. Bernard, Newfoundland, Pyrenean Mountain Dog, Bernese Mountain Dog, Bouvier Des Flandres, Alaskan Malamute and others, would be quite a handful for a junior to cope with. But there are always exceptions to the rule. Space can be limited in the show ring, particularly when it comes to moving your dog. But there must always be enough room to stand your dog for the judge's inspection, so make sure you don't get cramped up into a corner.

There is a special technique involved in exhibiting the coated dogs in the Gundog Group to their best advantage. These breeds include the Golden Retriever, the English Setter, Irish Setter, Gordon Setter and the Irish Red and White Setter, all of which have glamorous feathering to show off. The handler holds the dog's head up with one hand, encouraging it to look forward. The other hand should be used to raise the tail level with the back, ensuring that the abundant feathering on the tail is on view. It is not an easy technique to master, but it is a very impressive sight when negotiated properly. In fact, the smooth-coated gundogs also look good when they are handled in this way.

In the Hound Group, the glamorous looks of the Afghan take a lot of beating, especially when it is on the move, with its profuse coat flowing in the breeze. Unfortunately, they are quite a handful for a junior, along with the Borzoi, Bloodhound, Irish Wolfhound and the Deerhound. In the Utility Group, the Standard Poodle is an attractive dog to handle. The head should be held up to show its elegant outline, and the handler usually holds the tail up, taking hold of a little of the tail pom-pom. The problem comes with the movement, as the Standard Poodle must move freely with plenty of drive, and this might be difficult for a small child to keep pace with. The Leonburger, another member of this group, needs to be free standing; the gait is free and firm, and it needs a strong person to hold it.

In my experience, I have found the German Shepherd Dog is particularly responsive to commands. I would place the Belgian Shepherd Dog in the same category, along with the Rough and Smooth Collie. These are all big dogs that look striking in the show ring, and I have seen them handled by juniors with considerable success.

Chapter Nine

MOVING YOUR DOG

When the judge has examined the dog individually, either on the table or on the ground in the centre of the ring, he will ask the handler to move the dog in a triangle, or up and back in a straight line first and then ask for the triangle. But before the handler starts on either move, he must first follow the judge back to the table so that he has the whole length of the ring available. The dog's collar or chain needs to be in the right position on the dog's neck, and you should be holding the lead firmly as you start off, with the dog moving on your left side. If you have a large dog, its strides must be long and flowing. The handler must not attempt to slow the dog down and run slowly, as this makes the dog look uncoordinated. If you are moving a small dog, you must shorten your pace to match the dog's and establish a nice, coordinated rhythm. Move directly away from the judge, using as much control over the dog as possible. Try to stay calm and relaxed, as feelings can travel down the lead.

When you reach the first turn of the triangle, put your right hand under the dog's chin and assist it gracefully as the left turn is made. Then move out with the dog across the bottom of the ring, with your hand back at your side. When you come to the final turn, again place your right hand under the dog's chin and make a left turn, heading in a straight line back to the judge, with your right hand back at your side. When you have completed the triangle, stop and pose the dog about two metres from the judge, presenting the dog's side-view. Sometimes you will be asked to move the dog in a straight line away from the judge, and back again. The handler should move out gracefully, with the dog slightly in front or alongside. I prefer my dog to be at a 45 degree angle in front of me when I am moving. When you reach the top of the ring, give yourself enough time to move the dog around without stopping, and encourage it by calling its name. Then return to the judge and pose the dog about two metres away from him.

If the ring is not wide enough for the handler to move in a triangle, the judge will ask you to move the dog up and back twice, in a straight line. He will be assessing the rear and front action of the dog. The judge will then go to the left side of the ring and, looking from the judging table to the bottom of the ring, he will assess the side movement. Keep the dog on your left side, and move as briskly and smoothly as before. Just before making the about turn, pass the lead from the left hand to the right, as smoothly as possible, and continue moving, the dog on the right side, passing in front of the judge. When you have passed the judge, make an about turn to the right and change the lead to the left hand, so that the dog is on your left. Then stop in front of the judge and pose the dog. Try to look assured and confident. When you stop in front of the judge, do not look up as if to say: "What next?" Stop, pose the dog, bait it or make some gesture to encourage an alert expression, or slight tail-wagging to show a merry character. Then look at the judge with an expression that says: "Look no further, Judge, here is your winner!"

Before the judge makes his final choice, he might ask all the handlers to move their dogs once or twice around the ring in a circle. Make sure you don't crowd the handler in front or allow yourself to be crowded from behind. The best thing to do is to leave sufficient space in front, more than you require, and then if you are crowded you can move quickly into the space ahead. Do not allow your dog to over-shadow the dog in front, and make

Dog and handler turn to the left. This exercise is used so that the judge can asses rear action as the dog is moving away, and the front action as the dog returns. The golden rule is to always keep the dog between you, the handler, and the judge.

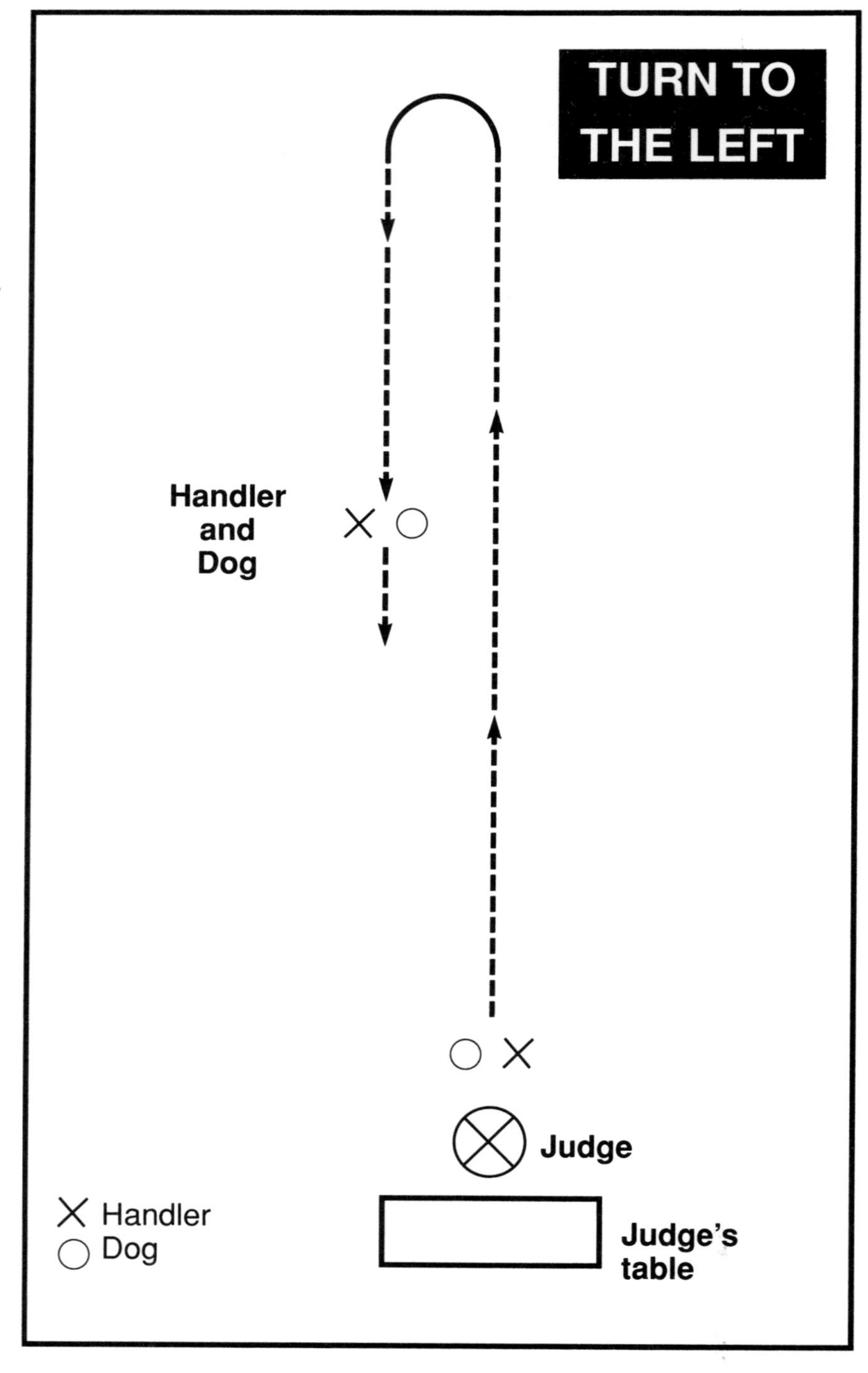

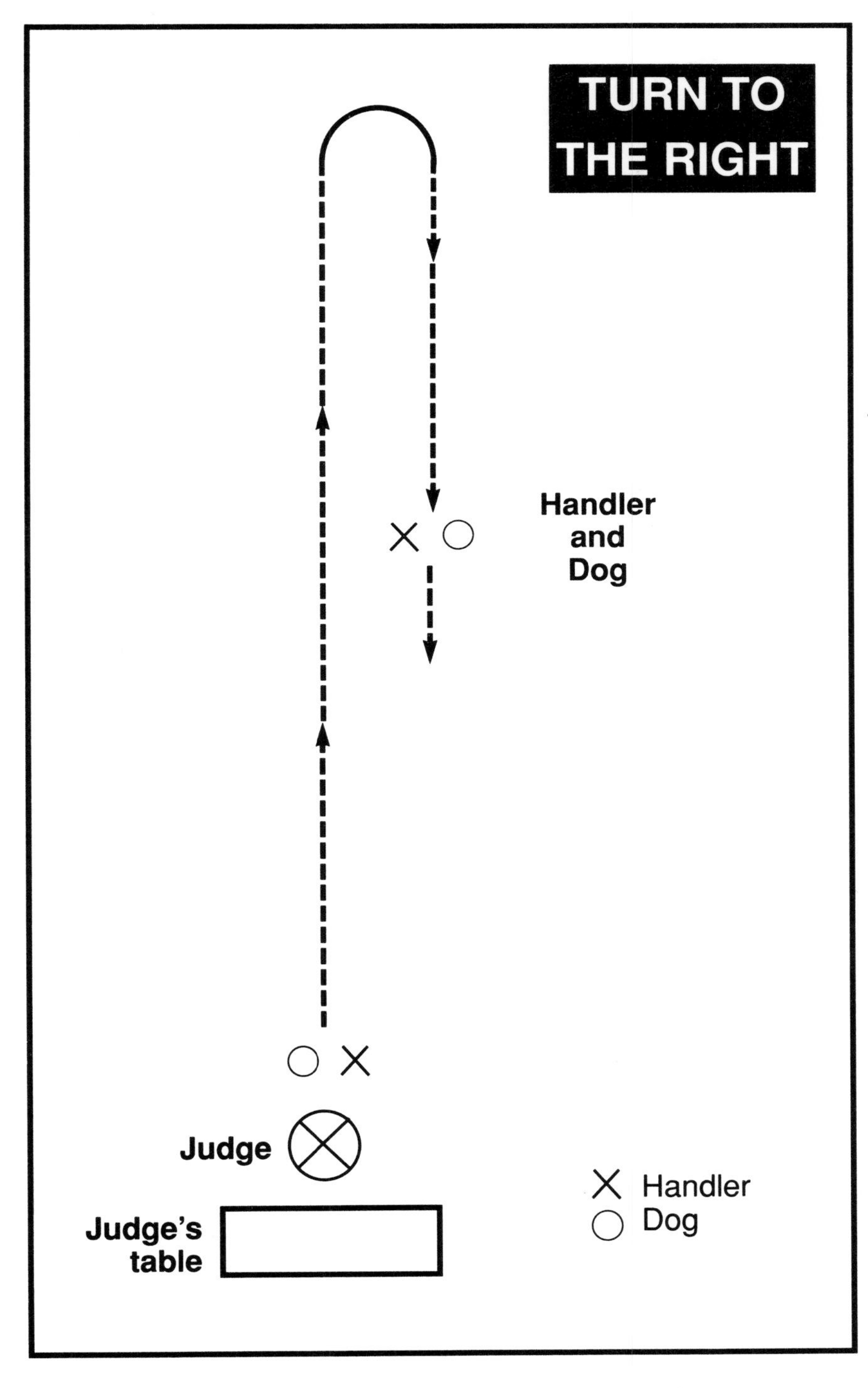

Dog and handler turn to the right. The method for this exercise is exactly the same as for the left turn, except some handlers prefer to turn to the right, allowing the dog to continue the flow of movement without a break. The dog is only obscured from the judge for a very short space of time, but unbroken movement can be noted. I do not penalise the right turn, as this exercise done well, allows the handler and dog a flowing turn about.

The dog should always be kept on the left of the handler. This exercise is used to assess the rear action of the dog as it moves away from the judge, the side action when it is moved from right to left, and the front action as it returns to the judge.

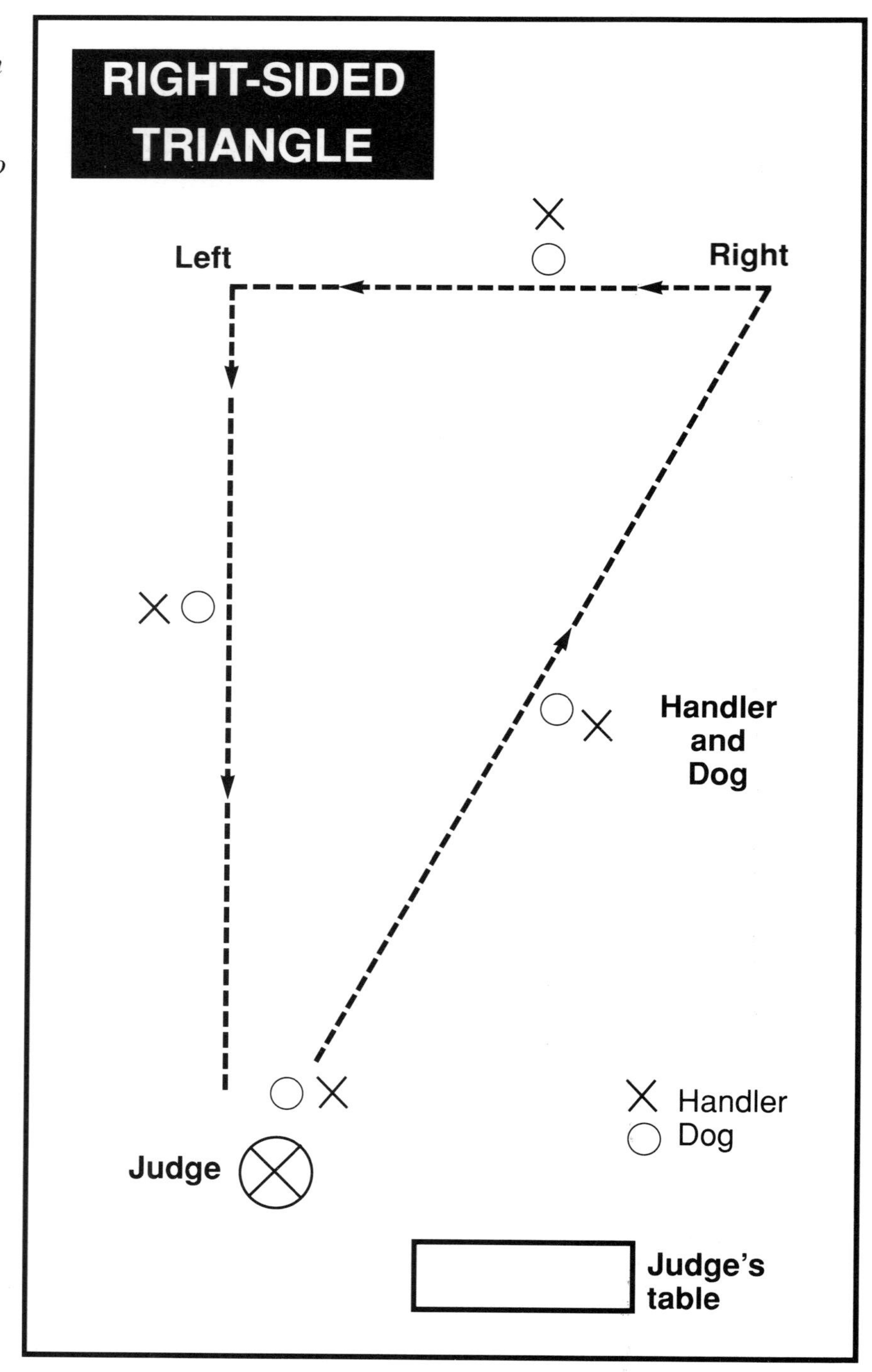

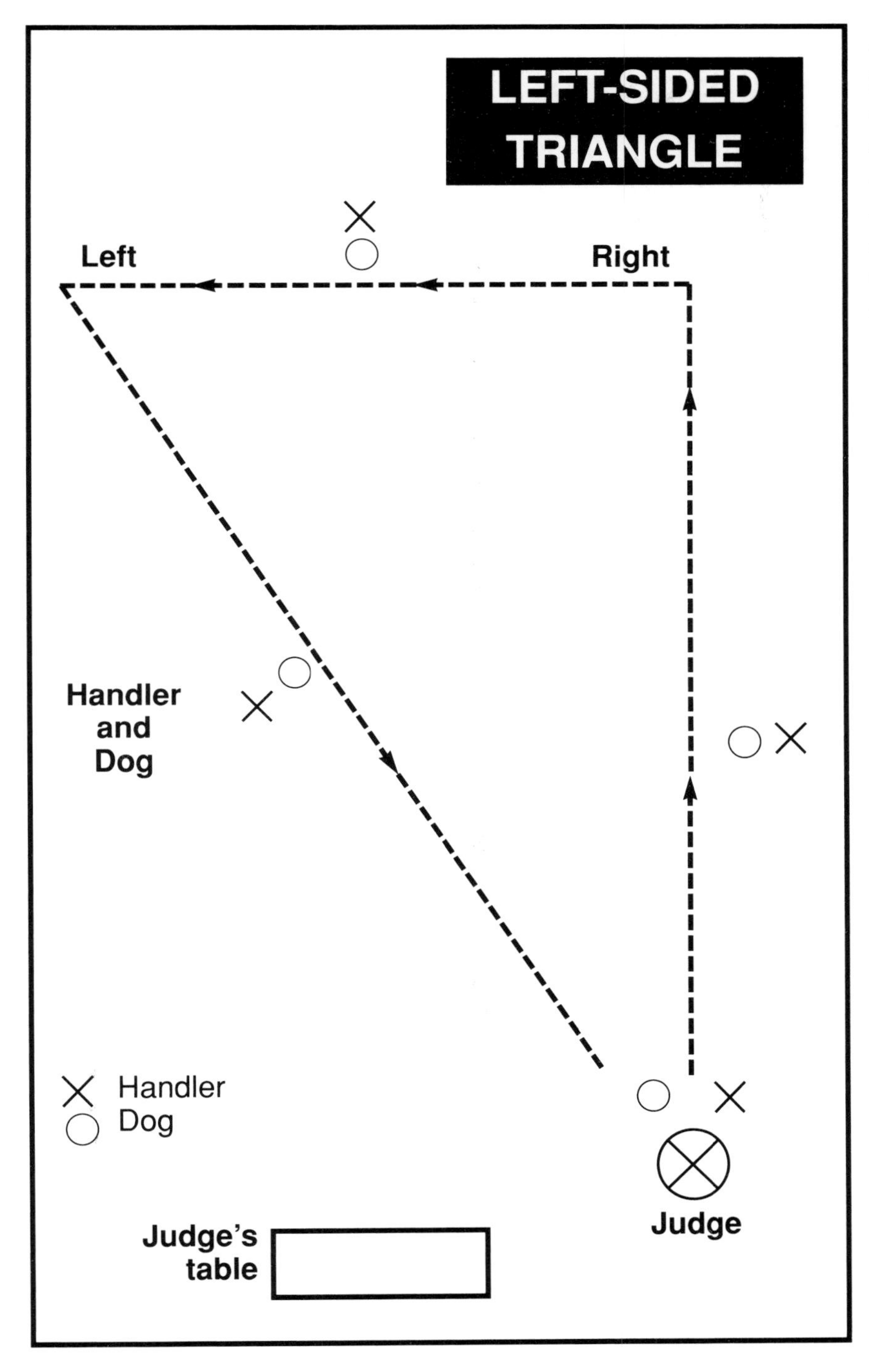

Exactly the same procedure is adopted as for the right-sided triangle, except the handler moves off in a straight line and then turns left.

This exercise is to assess rear, side and front movement. At the start of the exercise the handler should go to the front of the judge and move away, gaiting the dog, as illustrated.

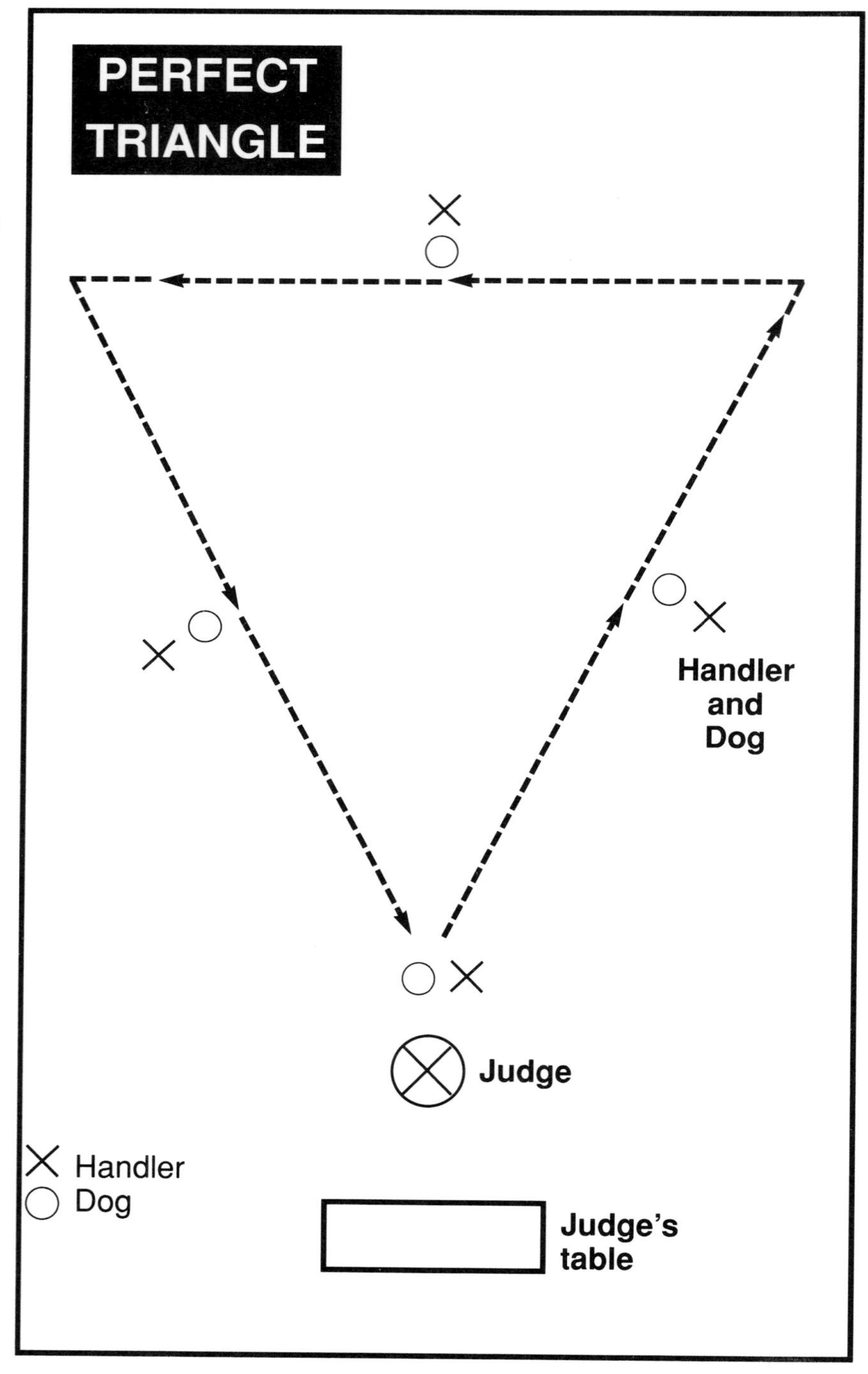

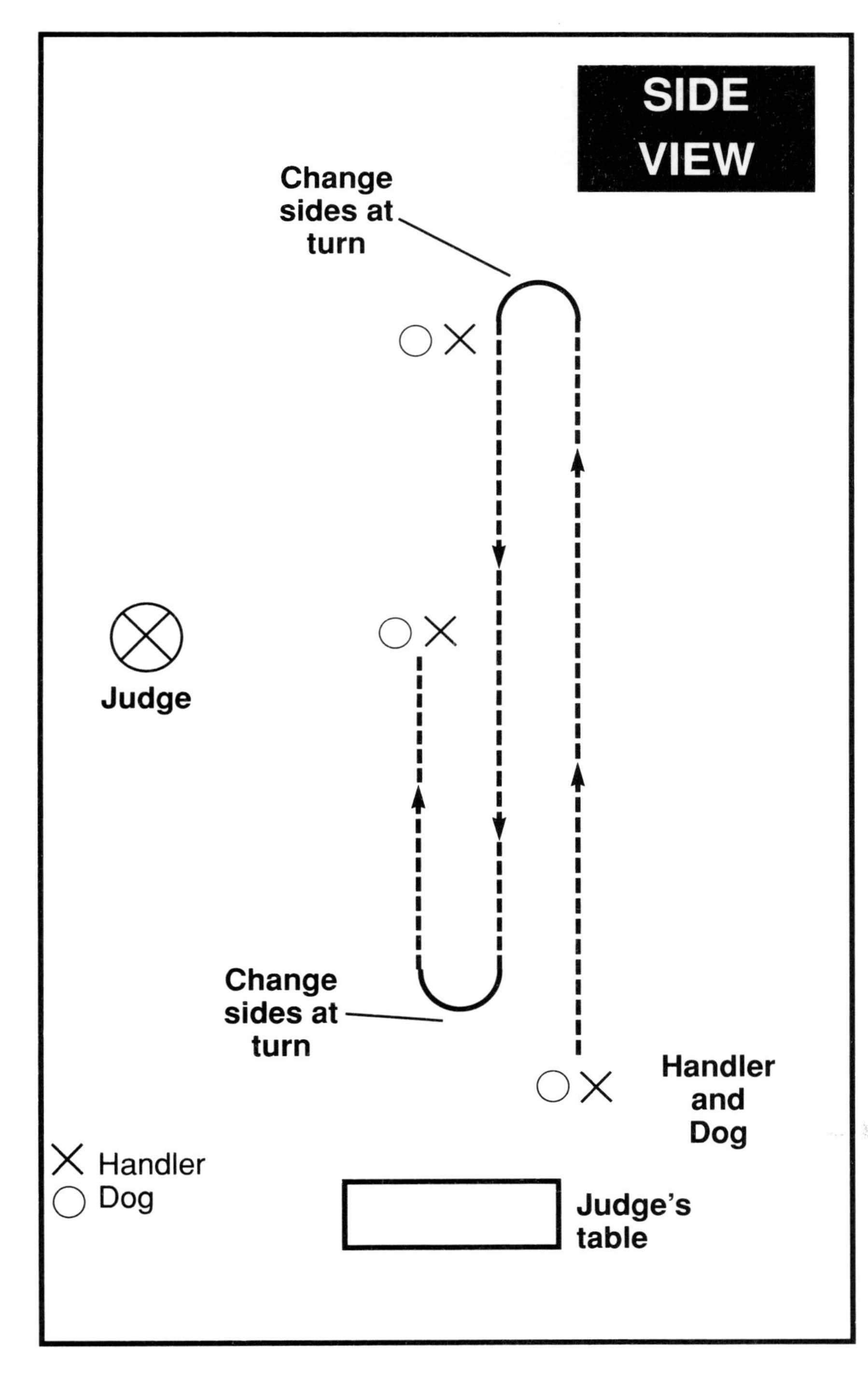

This method is used when the ring is not wide enough for the handler to move the dog in a circle or in a triangle. The judge goes to the side, to view side movement. When the handler reaches the end of the ring, he must make an about turn to the left, putting the lead in the right hand and keeping the dog on the right side, passing by in front of the judge. When the handler has passed the judge he should make an about turn to the right and change the lead to the left hand, so that the dog is on the left side. The handler should then stop in front of the judge and pose the dog.

This exercise is used to view the side gait of the dog. The dog should be on the left side of the handler, with the handler moving anti-clockwise, while the judge remains at the centre of the ring. When the judge asks the handler to stop, the dog should be posed for the judge to make the final assessment.

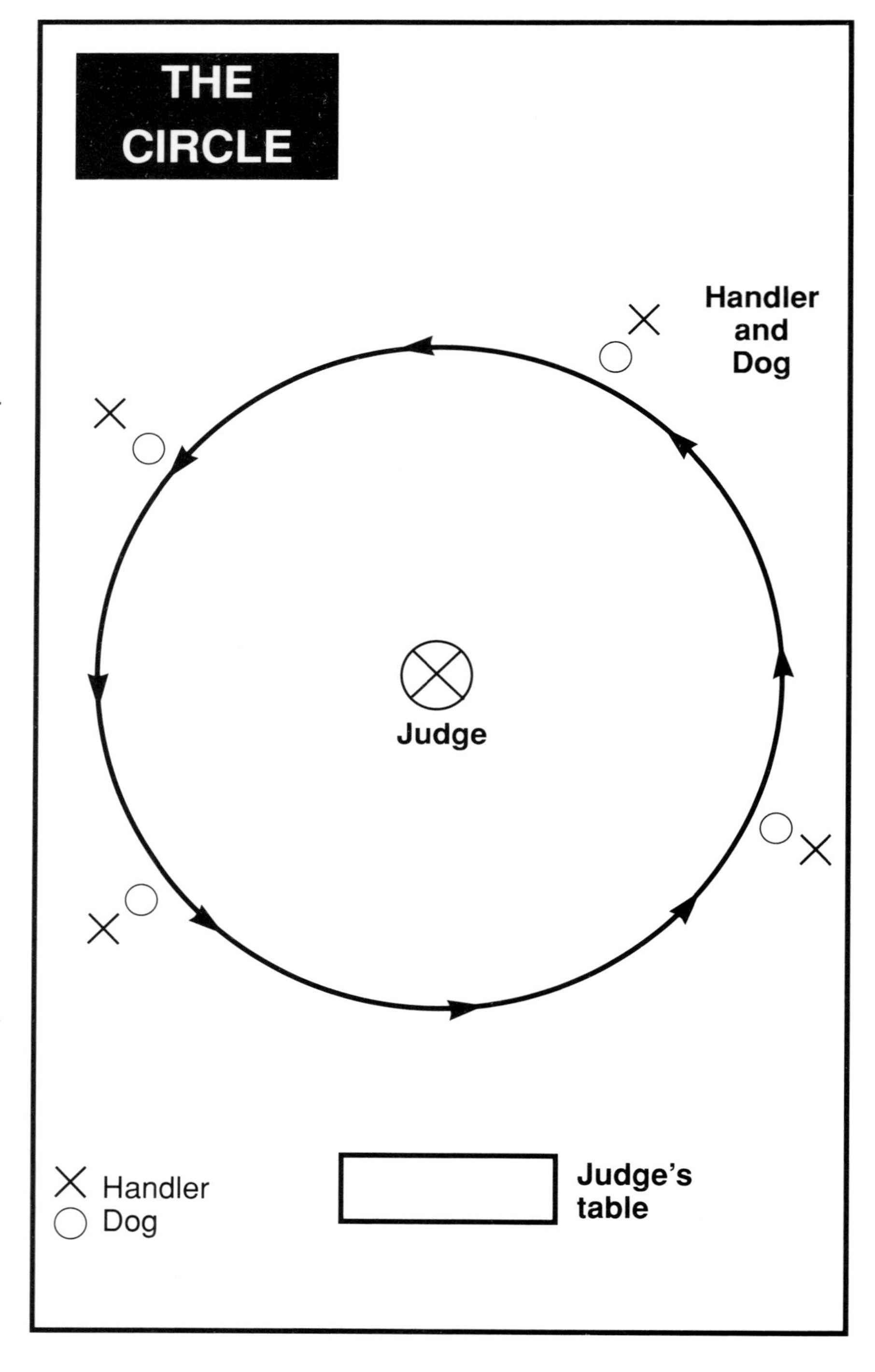

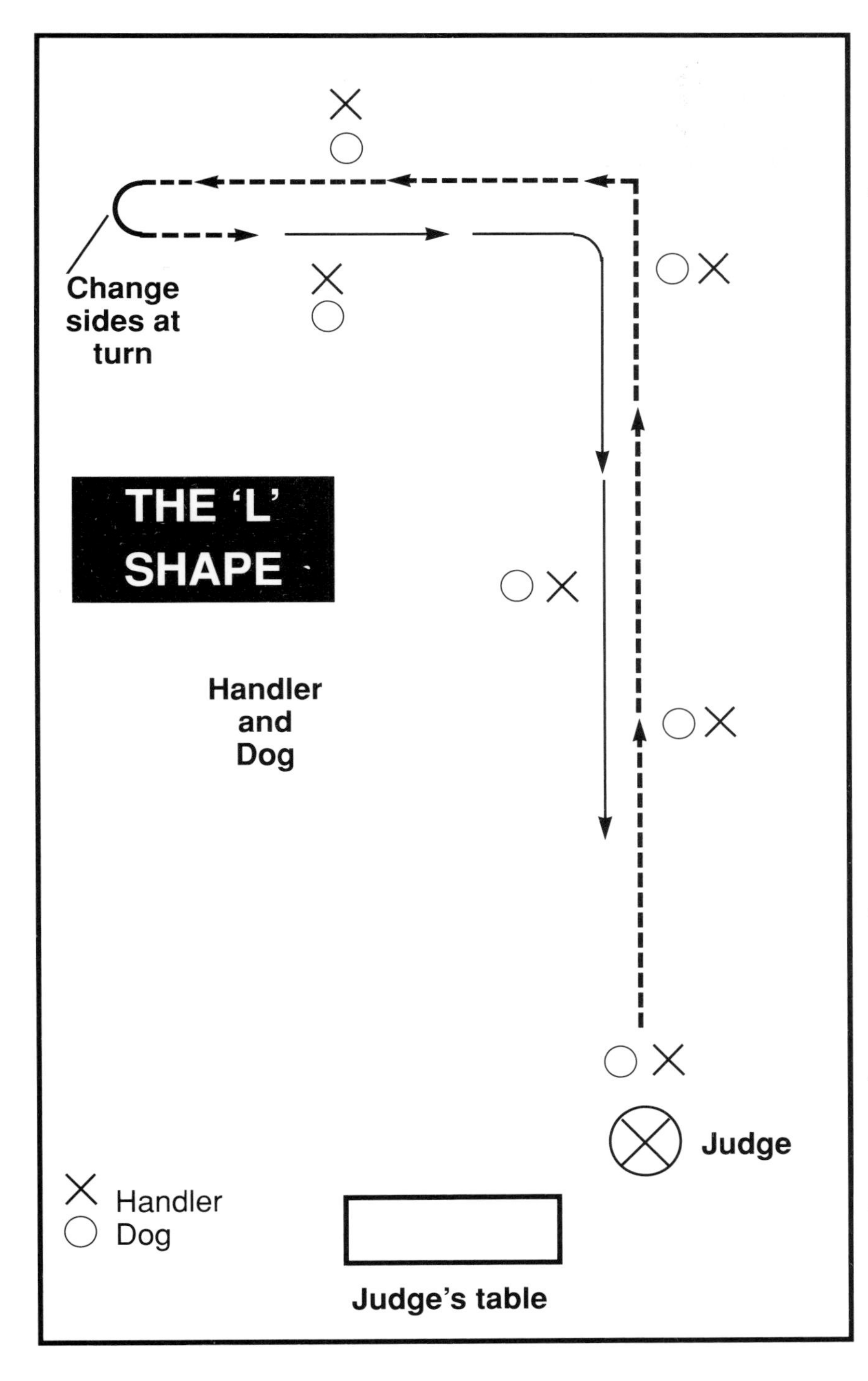

To perform the "L" exercise, the handler moves away from the judge with the dog on the left side. At the bottom of the ring, the handler takes a left turn. On reaching the left side of the ring, the handler should move the lead from the left hand to the right hand, then making an about turn to the left. The dog should be on the handler's right and heading to the other side of the ring. When level with the judge, the handler makes a right turn and heads back towards the judge. Finish by posing the dog about two metres in front of the judge.

The handler moves away from the judge with the dog on his left. At the bottom of the ring, he or she makes a left turn. At the left side of the ring, the handler should move the lead from the left hand to the right hand, making an about turn to the left. The dog should be on the handler's right and heading towards the other side of the ring. At the other side of the ring, the handler should move the lead from the right hand into the left, and make a right about turn to head for the opposite side of the ring. The dog should be on the left side. When level with the judge, the handler should make a left turn and head back towards the judge in a straight line, posing the dog about two metres in front of the judge.

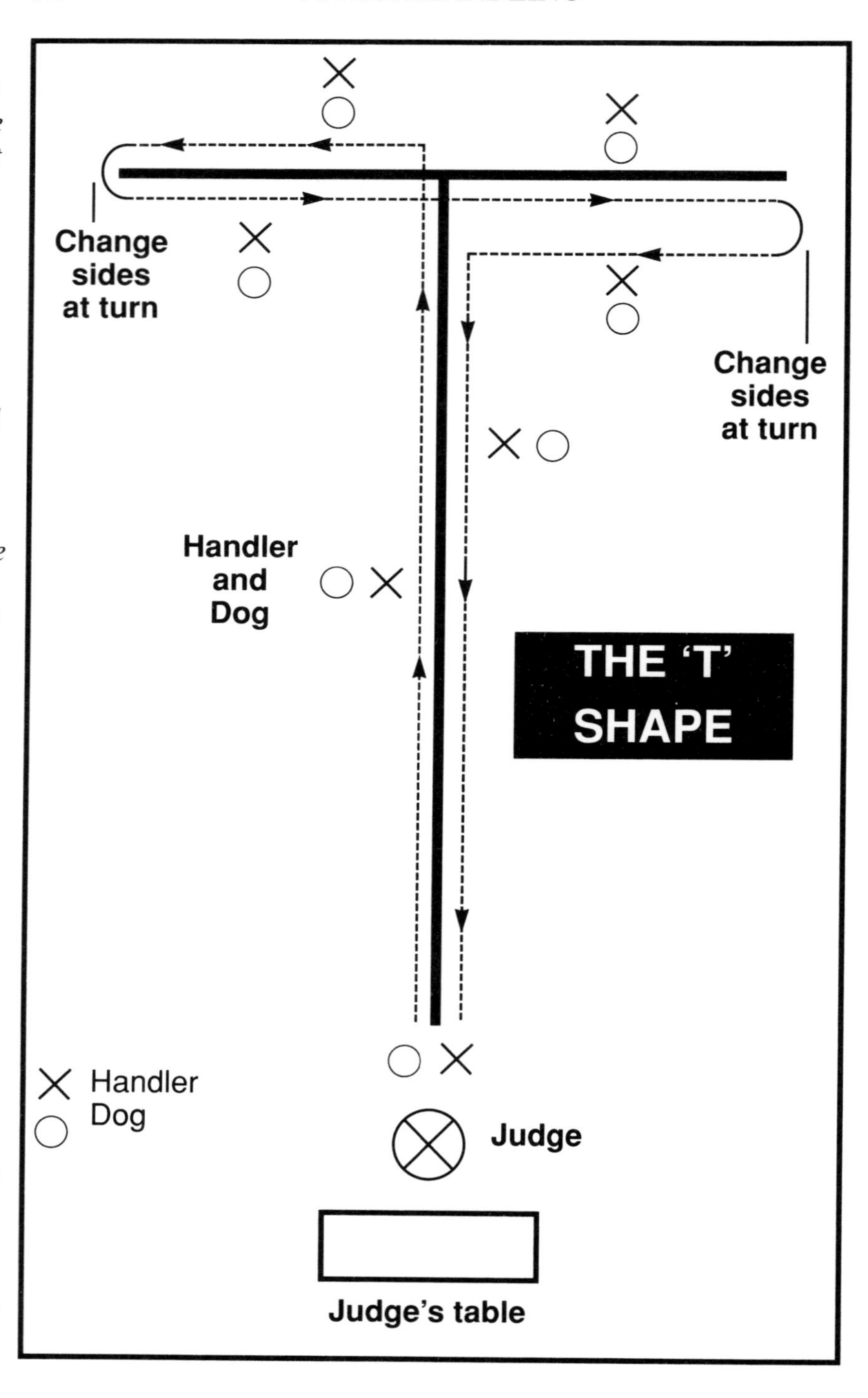

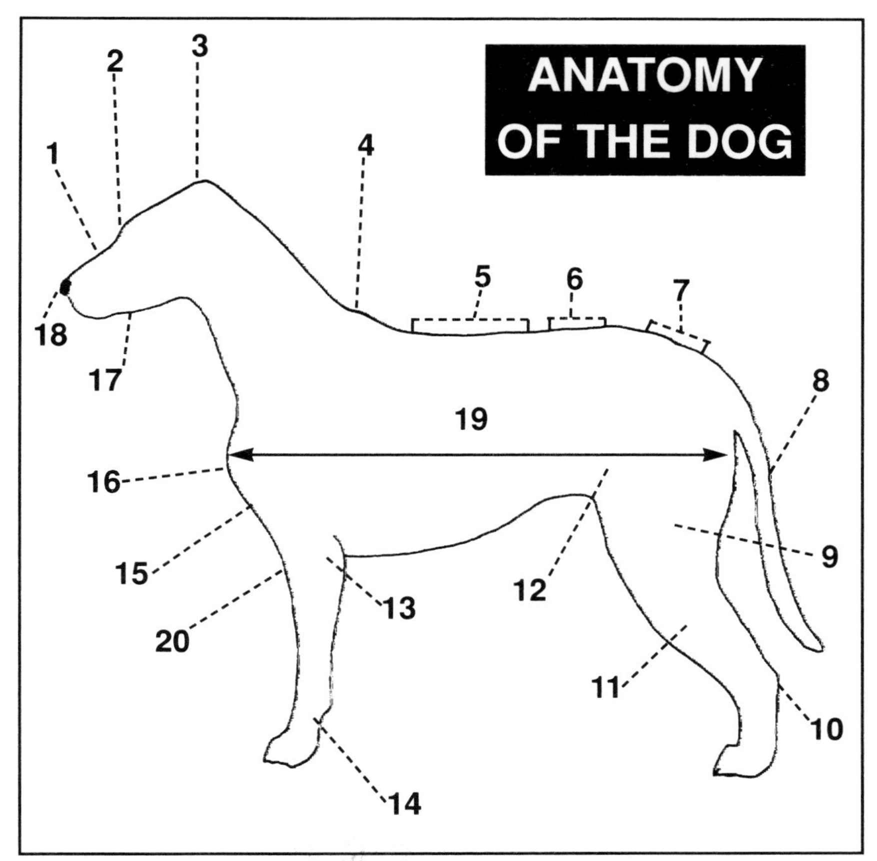

I never ask a junior handler technical questions in the ring. But I think it is important they understand the physique of a dog.

1	**Foreface or Muzzle**	11	**Stifle**
2	**Stop**	12	**Flank**
3	**Occiput**	13	**Elbow**
4	**Withers**	14	**Pastern**
5	**Back**	15	**Upper Arm**
6	**Loin**	16	**Point of shoulder**
7	**Croup**	17	**Underjaw**
8	**Tail**	18	**Nose**
9	**Thigh**	19	**Length of body**
10	**Hock**	20	**Brisket**

sure the person behind does not have the opportunity to overshadow your dog.

There are certain positions and manoeuvres that can be adopted as part of the training exercises, but I believe these are totally inappropriate when applied to the show ring. There is no value to be gained from asking a junior to negotiate certain letters of the alphabet. The most likely result is that the handler will become totally unnerved and confused. In my opinion, it is not a fair test of an individual's handling ability. In a training situation, navigating the different letters can help a handler to learn to control the dog. The letter T, though seldom used, can come in handy when there is insufficient room to do a triangle. The letter L is also suitable in these circumstances, so it is probably worth learning these two set pieces.

For the letter T, move away from the judge, with the dog on your left. When you reach the bottom of the ring, make a left turn. On reaching the left side of the ring, move the lead from your left hand to your right hand, making a left about-turn. The dog should be on your right, and heading towards the other side of the ring. When you reach the other side, repeat the procedure, this time moving the lead from your right hand to your left hand, making a right about-turn to head for the opposite side of the ring. The dog should be on your left side as you make a left turn in the middle of the ring, heading back to the judge in a straight line.

Again, I must emphasise that this is not a standard procedure, and in over twenty years of handling in America, Britain and on the Continent, I have only ever been asked to demonstrate a triangle, a circle, and going straight up and down the ring.

Chapter Ten

MATTERS OF OPINION

In America, judges must follow certain guidelines when they are judging junior handlers, but there is no equivalent code of practice in the United Kingdom. As a result, judges are left to decide for themselves what is a fair and acceptable system. This, I believe is far too haphazard an approach, and I hope it is something that will be rectified before too long. My procedure for judging juniors remains basically the same, whether I am officiating at an Exemption Show, an Open Show, a Championship Show, or even at the International Final. Situations may change, but the most important thing is to give the juniors the respect they deserve, regardless of age. They should be treated in exactly the same way as an adult in a breed class.

Entries at Open Shows and Championship Shows tend to be large, so I get the whole class assembled in the ring and split them into two halves, and then everyone has enough room to operate. I inform the ring steward that I want table dogs brought to the front, and the breeds are grouped together. This allows me to compare how the same breed is handled. I then go round the ring and inspect each handler and dog. This also gives the handlers a chance to settle their dogs. I then ask my steward to tell the handlers to relax, while I am busy examining each entry individually.

The first thing I look for is how the handler poses their dog, whether it is on the table or on the ground in the middle of the ring. If I am judging a table dog, I like the handler to pose it so that I can stand right in front of the dog and go over it, without having to reach across the table. I also want the handler to stand out of the way, so I do not feel crowded. The ideal place for the handler to stand is to the side, holding on to the lead. After I have inspected the dog, I watch as the handler lifts the dog from the table, and then I ask them to do the triangle.

The larger dogs should be posed in the middle of the ring so that I have plenty of room to stand in front of the dog and then walk round it. I always like to see a natural pose. By this I mean that the handler should allow the dog to position itself by walking into a posed stance. If this is not possible, I have no objection to seeing the exhibit set up by the handler, as long as it is done in a graceful manner. If the dog requires to be baited, the normal practice is for the handler to stand directly in front of the dog's head with the titbit. But as I approach, the handler should move slightly to the left or right to give me a clear view of the dog. When I have examined the front of the dog, I move round to the side, then to the rear. When I start to move, the handler should resume their first position at the dog's head. The most important thing to remember is never to stand between the judge and the dog. I then ask the handler to move the dog. First, I return to the judge's table, and I expect the handler to follow me and then wait until I am ready before setting off on the triangle. It seems obvious, but I have lost count of the times that a junior has set off while I have still had my back to them. At the end of the movement, the handler should pose the dog so I can make a final assessment, and then they should return to the line at the side of the ring. The steward will usually tell you where to go.

I do not expect dogs to be held in pose while I am going over other dogs. But it is wise to keep an eye on the judge, and periodically put the dog into pose, in case he glances in your direction. Some judges like to see the dogs held in a pose the whole time they are in the ring. But if it is a large class, I think it is very tiring for handlers and dogs alike. Some dogs actually resent being fussed all the time, having their feet placed in position and being set up, and as a result they start to fidget and become generally restless. If the dog is not put under too much stress, it will behave much better, and when you put the dog into a pose for the final assessment, it could make all the difference.

Dogs are not statues; they will not stand still all the time, and sometimes a dog will break a pose. A handler will not be penalised for this. But what I do expect to see is the handler responding in a calm, sensible manner, and putting the dog back into a pose with as little fuss as possible. I am always impressed to see a handler coping with a difficult situation with patience and determination. No dog should be chastised by its handler in the ring, or outside the ring, for misbehaving. The object of the exercise is to control the dog – not mistreat it. If the dog has failed to respond to commands, the answer is to practise more at home, and your dog should do better next time.

When there are ten or more entries to a class, I choose five handlers to assess again. I ask them to exchange dogs, or I pick two well-mannered dogs for them all to handle. I always ask each handler if they mind handling another breed of dog. I also ensure that the dog is sufficiently sweet-tempered to allow a stranger to handle it.

Some junior handlers have not been too happy about being judged by those that have no special interest in this aspect of the show world. Their complaints were voiced by Averil Cawthera-Purdy, who writes the junior handling column in the weekly dog paper, *Dog World*. At the same time, I approached Liz Cartledge, secretary of the Junior Handling Association, with a plan to draw up an official judging list. I drafted a list of requirements and prepared an application form for all those who felt they were suitably qualified. My aim was to make it direct and easy to understand, yet carrying sufficient weight and importance for it to be taken seriously. Liz Cartledge approved the draft, and following publicity in the junior handling column of *Dog World*, the application form was printed and the first judging list is being launched.

In the first week we received thirty-five applications and the

Junior Handling Association is now in the process of drawing up a Judges List which can be sent out when diplomas and entry forms are issued. Obviously, every judge has his own methods, and I would not want to interfere with the way an individual seeks out his ideal handler. But judges should remember that many of the juniors, especially in the younger age group, can be very easily over-awed, especially if the judge is well known. It can be like meeting Santa Claus for the first time: you have heard stories about how nice he is, but you still feel wary when you are invited to sit on his lap. Some juniors look as though they are in complete control and full of confidence, but they quiver and shake if something unusual happens. The age of their dog is on the tip of their tongue, but when a judge asks for the handler's age first, it is easy to get confused. That is why I think it is totally wrong to start asking questions about a dog's anatomy. That is not because I think juniors should not learn about it – I think it is very important to understand the physical make-up of a dog – but the show ring is not the place to start quizzing juniors, who already have enough on their mind in trying to get the best from their dog.

I believe the fairest way to judge juniors is to adopt more or less the same procedure that you would use for adults in the breed ring, with a few allowances for inexperience. The last thing you want to do is to make the whole competition into a game to catch the junior out. This will not help anybody. It is also important to remember that the judge is also on trial. The juniors of today could well be the judges of tomorrow, and so a judge of junior handling must be above reproach in both his method and behaviour. Make no mistake, the importance of the juniors is growing all the time. I believe that in the not too far distant future their involvement in the dog world will be so great it will warrant a two-day event staged exclusively for them, covering all aspects of dog training from show ring handling to obedience and agility. As far as I am concerned, that day cannot come soon enough.

JUNIOR HANDLING ASSOCIATION JUDGING APPLICATION FORM

The Junior Handling classes must be judged and assessed on the proficiency of the young handlers who are demonstrating their ability to control a dog as if it is being exhibited in Breed Competition.

Judges should bear in mind that it is not the quality of the dog that is being judged, but rather the competence and skill of the handler.

Any person that is qualified to judge at Open or Championship Shows will be eligible to judge the Junior Handling classes providing they comply with the following requirements.

OPEN/CHAMPIONSHIP SHOWS

a. Must have shown an interest in all aspects of Junior Handling.
b. To judge the Junior Handling Association qualifying classes applicants must have two years or more experience judging a breed, or breeds at Open or Championship level.
c. Judges who have already judged JHA classes and comply with a and b.

Please include a summary of judging experiences for breed and/or Junior handling.
This information will be forwarded as a list to the JHA co-ordinator Mrs Liz Cartledge.

EXEMPTION, SANCTION, LIMITED and non-qualifying JH classes at OPEN SHOWS

1. To judge non qualifying classes at Open Shows, applicants must have had one year of judging experience.
2. Applicants with less than one year of judging experience.
3. Applicants that have been active as Junior handling exhibitors and who are over the age of 17.

Chapter Eleven

TIPS FROM THE TOP

Marita Rodgers proves that success as a junior can lead to greater things in the dog world. She is now a highly respected judge and handler, and she judged the national Junior Handler of the Year final in 1988. Marita Gibbs, as she was in her junior handling days, had her first experience of the show ring when she was still in her carrycot! Her mother breeds the world famous Montravia Poodles and Afghans, and so it was not surprising that Marita was steeped in the dog world from a tender age. She started handling dogs for her mother, and when she was only ten years old she won a first prize in a breed class. This was the first in a long line of successes, but she particularly remembers her first challenge certificate and Best of Breed award at Crufts with her Toy Poodle Ch. Montravia Spring Flamenco. When she was in her teens, Marita started competing in junior handling classes, which were then organised by the Dog Centre in Birmingham, and she came second in the national final in two consecutive years. In fact, she failed to pick up a first prize in junior handling, despite handling six champions by the time she was nineteen years old. "This is something I always tell youngsters, when they are complaining that they cannot win, no matter how hard they try," says Marita.

Marita, who won Best In Show at Crufts in 1983 with an Afghan and again in 1985 with a Standard Poodle, has now judged junior handling semi-finals and final, and her advice is well worth listening to. When she judges juniors, she expects them to complete all the exercises that are required in the breed classes.

"The thing I look for is an affinity between the dog and the handler," she says. "I believe a dog will give its best if it is handled gently and kindly by a sympathetic handler. Someone who has a natural sympathy with dogs is also at an advantage when a change of dogs is required. They will have a dog co-operating with them, even though they have only had a few minutes to get to know the dog."

Marita suggests that juniors get to know as many breeds as possible, before they reach the top level of competition, and then they will know the correct style of handling to adopt.

"When you are asked to handle a dog that you are not familiar with, you cannot expect it to co-operate immediately. But you will achieve results if you use a little gentle persuasion. Jerking or yanking the lead will be no help whatsoever. I have always found that breeds in the Hound Group are particularly susceptible to heavy handling. They become nervous and uncontrollable. I once handled an Afghan who had been roughly treated and it took me a very long time to settle the dog, and only after hours of training would it co-operate in the show ring. The best technique is to spend time talking to the dog and coaxing it while you are putting on a collar and lead, then to follow it wherever it wants to go. Then, start persuading the dog to follow you, and you will find that your patience has paid off.

"Never be afraid to make a fuss of your dog when your are in the show ring. The dog will respond and the judge will see that you have a good rapport with it."

The one thing that upsets Marita is seeing juniors pushed into competitions by their parents, rather than because they want to get involved in handling.

"A junior will never do well under that sort of pressure," she says. "The child will probably start to resent dog shows and the

Vince Mitchell: Judge of the 1987 Junior Handler of the Year, campaigning the Wire Fox Terrier.

Cooke.

whole dog world after a while. Equally, parents should never expect too much from their children. I once saw a mother ranting and raving because her child had only come second in a huge class. The child was terribly upset, and the whole family left the show immediately. Needless to say, that youngster has never been to a show again."

Vince Mitchell judged the Junior Handler Final in 1987, and like Marita he has lived and breathed dogs since he was born. His father Billy was a well known breeder of Wire Fox Terriers and a professional handler. Vince handled his first Best in Show when he was only six years old and he went on to become a professional handler, piloting some famous dogs to their titles and winning many Groups and Best in Show awards. When he was being paid to handle dogs in America and in Britain, he would insist that he had the dog in his care long before the day of the show, in order to groom it and train it to perfection.

"When I went into the show ring, I was always aiming to win the Group, and the Best in Show," he says. "You must always believe in yourself and give one hundred per cent."

He likes to see juniors show competence and control, without being too showy.

"I try to judge juniors in a very straightforward way," he says. "After all, we are all trying to assess good, practical handling; we are not trying to put on a circus act."

He gives his directions clearly and concisely, and the only question he asks is the dog's age. He goes over the dog as thoroughly as if he was judging a breed class, but all the time he is judging the individual's handling ability.

"I have seen some judges who have asked the handlers to do impossible tricks," he says. "They have moved the dog's feet out of position, and then expected the handler to immediately pose the dog correctly again. At the same time they have been firing questions at the handler, which are not relevant to the job in hand. The result is that both the dog and the handler get confused, and it is impossible to tell whether they have any true handling skills.

"I like to see a junior that is well presented and shows good overall knowledge and handling technique. The worst fault I have seen is when juniors try to make too much of a show of themselves and show too many mannerisms in the way they handle the dog."

Carolyn Whitlock, known in her junior handling days as Carolyn Craig, started off by handling her mother's Labrador Retrievers and then moved on to Miniature Schnauzers. Her first major success was when her own Schnauzer, Balmar Silver Cracker, was made up to a champion. Carolyn is now qualified to judge Labradors, Miniature Schnauzers, Schnauzers and Giant Schnauzers at challenge certificate level, and she is closely involved with junior handlers. She has judged the International Junior Handler classes in Jersey for three consecutive years. Like Marita Rodgers, Carolyn looks for an affinity between handler and dog.

"Those handlers that are working in close unison with their dogs stand out a mile," she says. "That is very important, because the judge only has a few minutes to assess the individual skills of a handler. These days, juniors have become so professional, it gets increasingly hard for judges to make a decision.

"I expect handlers to go through the same exercises as would be expected in the breed classes; they don't need to perform extra tricks."

Carolyn broke with the traditional format when she was judging the UK finals at Birmingham. She asked the handlers in her final line-up to take their dogs up the ring, two at a time, before making her final decision. She then moved to the side, and expected the handlers to move one dog slightly in front of the other, so that she could see the side view of each dog, rather than one dog obscuring the other.

"I expect handlers to show the bite of their dog without any assistance from me," she says. "The handler should lift up the dog's head so that I can see their mouth. When I am looking at a table dog, the handler should move so I have free access to the dog.

"I always ask the name and age of the dog that is being handled, and when a junior is told to swap dogs I expect them to know what breed it is, as this shows a serious interest in all aspects of dog handling.

" I am very quick to penalise a junior that is cruel to their dog or that handles it too roughly. This applies particularly in the use of the lead or choke chain. I also believe in keeping an eye on the handlers in the line-up, while I am doing my individual inspections. I think it keeps everyone on their toes. But most of all, I think dogs and handlers should enjoy the show ring, and win or lose, they should look forward to the next competition."

Louise Amos with the family dogs.

Louise teaching Fly the 'send away'.

Chapter Twelve

ANGLES ON HANDLING

In the ten years I have been judging junior handling classes I have met a number of youngsters who have gone on to become active in the breed ring. Invariably, they have found their early experience of immense value. Some juniors are highly competitive and their great ambition is to reach the final of the International Handler of the Year and compete at Crufts. Others simply enjoy the chance to work with their dog and get some useful experience of the show ring.

LOUISE AMOS

"My very first memory with dogs was sitting in the car on a freezing cold day with the rain pelting down, waiting for my Mum to carry out a tracking exercise with her dog Sweep," said Louise. "I must have been five or six years old at the time, but I didn't take an active interest in the showing side of dogs. I was pony-mad and gymkhanas were more my scene. But dogs were always part of my life. I learnt to walk by hanging on to our German Shepherd Dog's coat.

"My Mum started to take an interest in showing after entering

Sweep in a show class at the Border Collie Club's Obedience Show and taking Reserve Best in Show. This was before Border Collies were given Championship status. At the same time a scruffy little rescue bitch appeared on the scene and Mum agreed to help out and take her in temporarily. This was Fly, and she turned out to be my first Border Collie.

"Fly has the most unbelievable temperament. I made my debut with her in the show ring. We didn't make much of an impact, but we started doing well in junior handling classes because the dog doesn't have to be a fantastic show specimen. She was so laid back she was easy to handle and I could concentrate on looking good. That is what I thought at the time, but it was all going to change.

"In my second year of showing I qualified for the semi-finals at Richmond, but Fly came into season the day before the competition. At the last minute I decided to take Sweep into the ring. Sweep was difficult to handle; he fidgeted, refused to move and growled at the other dogs. I had to work really hard to make him co-operate. When we were pulled out into first place I could hardly believe it. Sweep was the first Border Collie (and is still the only one) to qualify for the JHA finals.

"The finals were held in the Metropole Hotel in Birmingham in January. When we arrived I was overawed by the glitter of the occasion. There were benches with dogs' names printed on them and real grass laid in one room for exercising the dogs. Everyone was dressed to the nines. I wore a white shirt and kilt, and I felt very humble as Sweep and I entered the green-carpeted ring under the chandeliers. Geoff Corish was judging, but despite Sweep's unusually impeccable behaviour we didn't get further than the first round. That day is one I will never forget – a brilliant occasion and an experience I thoroughly enjoyed. An interesting footnote to this was that the next day I went to a local show and wasn't even placed in a JHA class. It just goes to show that you can be up there at the top one day, and right back at the bottom the next.

"I never really had the chance to show a good dog in the breed ring until one year at Crufts Mum asked me to show Luc, our champion Groenendael, in his own class. Would I? Just try and stop me! It was a very useful experience and we finished by coming fifth. The next major win came when I was twelve and Mum allowed me to take Laird, our Border Collie, into his big post-graduate class at Builth Wells and he won, qualifying for Crufts. Meanwhile, Fly had produced some puppies, and I kept one, called Jack, to show. He won his puppy class at Richmond, qualifying for Crufts, where he also won his class. At the Ladies Kennel Association show that year my Groenendael dog Ben won his limit class and went on to win a reserve challenge certificate – another unforgettable moment. I remember shaking as the judge approached me to give me the reserve ticket and hugging her and crying afterwards. Some people thought I over-reacted, but it was a very special moment for me.

"When the Kennel Club Junior Organisation was formed I became a founder member and it opened up a lot of possibilities. I had never considered competitive obedience, but attending training clubs had given me some sort of groundwork and Fly was quite good at it. I read about the KCJO test of obedience and the search for a team to compete at Crufts. At the last minute I decided to have a go, but I had to teach Fly the 'send away' first. To my surprise, we made the team. We came a creditable fourth and I was seventh overall.

I still kept up with the junior handling and I remember one class when Felix Cosme was judging. It was an Open Show and I was competing alongside my friend Jenny. When it came to the stage where we had to swap dogs, Felix asked us to swap with each other. Unfortunately, he spotted the gleeful expressions on our faces and as a penance I ended up with an Afghan Hound... In the challenge for best handler I was given an enormous German Shepherd Dog which threw up clawfuls of rubber mat in its eagerness to drag me across the ring. Perhaps I gave the impression of complete control because Felix gave me the Best Handler Award.

"Now I am too old to compete at junior level, but I still take a keen interest in the classes and I love judging them. I feel I can pass on my experience, and I can honestly say that what you learn in junior handling pays off when you go on and show dogs in the breed ring."

DRYSTON FURBY

"My interest in dogs is something I have developed over the last three or four years," said Dryston. "Before that I was the cute little kid with the big hairy dog that was dragged backwards and forwards, despite any efforts on my part. I was taken to several dog shows by my parents, and then I began to take notice of what actually took place inside and outside the show ring. I soon found myself not only watching the Bearded Collies, which my family showed under the Pepperwood prefix, but I also took note of many other breeds, especially at Open Shows."

Pepperwood Dusky Night Dancer was the first dog Dryston handled and he did very well, even beating his mother when she was handling another of their Bearded Collies. He soon got involved in junior handling and qualified for the Richmond semi-finals when I was judging. He was in the huge Working Group, where there were some ninety entries to be judged. I split them into three groups and Dryston got through to the final line-up. I then asked the handlers to swap dogs and Dryston was given a Great Dane. I told him to go up the ring and return.

"Off I went," said Dryston. "Then suddenly, the dog hit its brakes and ran backwards. Felix saw the dog was too skittish, and so I was given a German Shepherd. I had had experience at training classes with German Shepherds and so it only took me a couple of steps before I was able to pace my movement with the dog's. The final choice was made and I finished third.

"I think that the standard of junior handling is improving all the time, but I think it is disheartening that the Working Group is so large, when you compare it to the small Terrier Group."

Dryston is now a judge of junior handling classes at Open Show level.

SHELDON FURBY

Sheldon's best friend when he was young was a black Labrador. "Dogs have always been in the family," he said. "I went to dog shows with my parents, first to watch and later to compete in obedience trials and in the show ring. There was one occasion when I wandered away from the Horse Ring at a big show and found my way to the Dog Show. I borrowed a dog to enter a

Sheldon Furby with Pepperwood Star Eclipse.

class, and my parents, frantic with worry, heard an announcement on the public address system: 'Will Mr and Mrs Furby please collect their son Sheldon from the Dog Show ring, where he has just been placed first.' I think the class was for 'the waggiest tail'."

Sheldon's brother Dryston was often competing at the same show, and on occasions Sheldon would win the six-to-eleven class and Dryston would win the twelve-to-sixteen class, so they would have to battle against each other for the Best Overall Handler. Sheldon qualified for the Richmond semi-finals in 1986 with his Bearded Collie, Pepperwood Star Eclipse, and the judge was Miss Beverly Cuddy.

"She really made us work hard," said Sheldon. "We had to keep gaiting the dogs to assess continuity – we couldn't relax for a minute. I was made Best Handler of the Working Group and so I went on to compete in the finals. That was a memorable day and I learnt a lot from the experience."

Sheldon, who is also a keen horse-rider, is still competing in junior handling classes in the upper age-group.

MAY-LISS MILLARD

May-Liss is fifteen years old and has been involved in junior handling since she was ten. The family have two Bearded Collies, Dusty of Melville, known as Dusty, and Wellknowe Patience, who is known as Kylie. May-Liss first started showing Dusty but she found him too boisterous. "I thought it was unfair on the other handlers in the class when they had to change dogs because Dusty got so excited," she said. Their next dog, Muffin, was easier to handle and May-Liss qualified for the Richmond semi-finals on a number of occasions.

"When I am changing dogs in the junior handlers class I like to have a little time to get to know the dog," she said. "I like to walk it up and down a few times before I have to show it to the judge. When I am in the ring I watch the other competitors to see how they handle the different breeds, just in case I am given a breed I am not familiar with. It is also a useful way of picking up tips from the other handlers."

VICTORIA FOX

Victoria started handling in September 1983 when she was thirteen years old, and in just twelve months she was awarded first place at the Richmond semi-finals under judge John Nicholls. She handled both West Highland White Terriers and Lhaso Apsos. In 1984 Victoria qualified for Richmond six times, and at the finals she was in the last six, becoming the top Utility handler of the year. The following year she was unplaced at Richmond despite qualifying twelve times, but she made up for it the next year when she qualified eighteen times and was placed fourth in the semi-finals. In 1987 Victoria was in her last year as a junior and she finished in third place at the semi-finals.

"The main dog I handle now is a Lhaso Apso called Darolam Brandy Boy, known as Bernard. I have won Best in Show, Best Puppy in Show and many Best of Breeds, including a Stud Book entry, with Bernard.

"I really enjoyed my time as a junior handler, and I am now a judge of junior handling classes. The experience also helped me to decide on my chosen career as a head veterinary nurse."

Victoria Fox with Darolam Brandy Boy.

TRACEY ALEXANDER

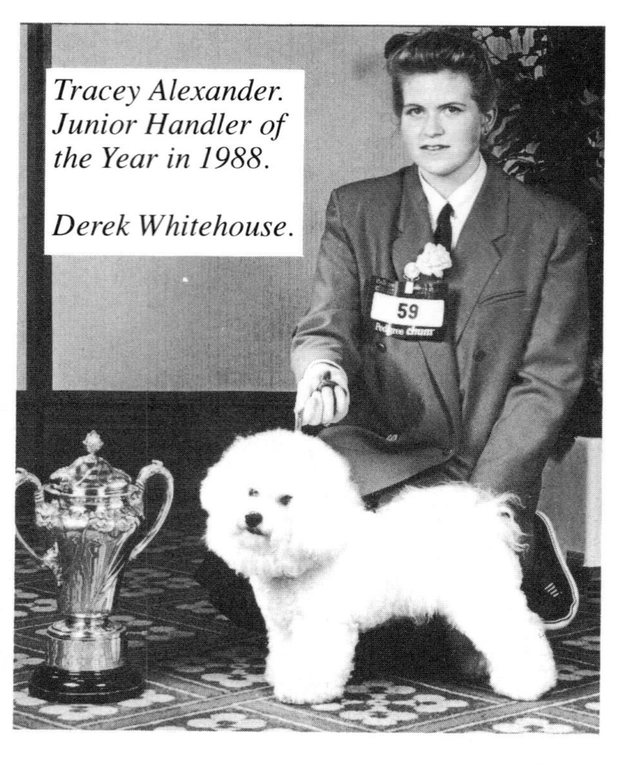

Tracey Alexander. Junior Handler of the Year in 1988.

Derek Whitehouse.

Tracey grew up with dogs, but although her mother showed dogs, the children were not really involved.

"My oldest sister Tamara used to help her," said Tracey. "But she did not like Sarah, Christopher and me going to shows, as we just used to get in the way. That all changed when I got to about twelve years old and my mother bought two puppies. Tamara had lost interest in showing and as my mother couldn't show two dogs at the same time I offered to help."

Since then dogs and dog-showing have been the main concern of Tracey's life. Her first involvement in junior handling came in 1985 when she started competing with a home-bred Bichon Frise named William.

"I entered every junior handling class I could in order to qualify for the semi-finals," said Tracey. "Eventually I qualified at an Open Show at Ardingly. That was not just a matter of luck, it took me time to improve my technique and I learnt a lot from watching other handlers."

Success came in the Kennel Club Junior Organisation competition, and Tracey was also a team member in the international handling competition in Jersey. In 1988 she qualified for the Junior Handler of the Year final in Birmingham and she won the title under judge Marita Gibbs.

"When I was competing in the final I was shaking with fright," said Tracey. "You can imagine what I felt like when I had to compete at Crufts against seventeen other handlers from different countries, with hundreds of spectators looking on."

I placed her third. She left her nerves outside the ring and gave a brilliant demonstration in handling. Tracey's junior handling career has now come to an end, but she is still deeply involved in the show world. She grooms dogs full time, takes on judging appointments and gives advice in a monthly column for *Our Dogs* Junior Special.

Mary Court (left) with her sister Sarah, her parents and their Rough Collies Paddy, Sandy, Rockie and Scott.

MARY COURT

Mary started showing dogs when she was six years old, competing with the family's Rough Collie called Paddy. She went to Exemption Shows and had her first win just before her seventh birthday. She then progressed to handling Alveston Royal Scott in all his breed classes and to date she has won three Best of Breed awards. A number of judges have commented on her outstanding ability, competing on a par with adult handlers. One judge, Ray Arthur, said: "She must be one of the best junior handlers in the country. I was particularly impressed by the way she emphasised the dog's good points, where so many adults show you all the bad points." In 1987 Mary qualified for the Richmond semi-finals twice, but was unable to attend. In 1988 she qualified ten times and reached the final sixteen from a total of seventy-two entries. 1989 proved to be a year to remember as Mary won the six to eleven year old class at Championship Shows four times, as well as being the Best Junior Handler at the West of England Collie Society's Championship Show. Unfortunately she could not go on to compete in the Richmond semi-finals as she came down with chicken pox. But there was some compensation when she was presented with the Treetops Shield, awarded to the junior with the most wins during the year. Mary had accumulated a grand total of twenty-four wins.

"I mostly handle our family's Rough Collies, but I enjoy handling other breeds as well," said Mary. "I hope to be a professional handler when I am older. I think it is important that junior handling is taken seriously; we should have good judges who are interested in this area. I think it is unfair when judges start assessing the dog, and not the ability of the handler."

Andrew Baker, Junior Handler of the Year 1987, with Ch. Ardessa Emerald Isla.

Dave Freeman.

Mary's little sister Sarah, aged six, is now taking an interest in junior handling and Mary is helping to teach her the basic procedures. She has already started winning classes handling a Shetland Sheepdog called Shellie.

ANDREW BAKER

Andrew is thirteen years old and has been handling since he was seven. His favourite breed is the Airedale Terrier, and when he was eleven he made up Champion Ardessa Emerald

Isla. In 1987 he won the Junior Handler of the Year under judge Vincent Mitchell, a terrier handler with an outstanding reputation. "My ambition is to handle top-class terriers and eventually to judge," said Andrew.

He has handled Sealyhams for Biddy Postgates and Airedales from Vanessa Johnson's Ardessa kennels. The hallmark of his style is confidence, composure and maturity.

"I greatly admire the handling skills of Geoff Corish, Mary Swash and Don Monro," said Andrew. "I have also had a tip or two from Fred Sills.

"There are certain aspects of junior handling competitions which I am not that keen on. At its worst it can be compared to sequence dancing. For example, sometimes a handler goes unnoticed, although he is showing a dog to perfection, simply because he does not have a flashy style and prefers to concentrate on the dog. The best thing is when the experienced junior handlers go on to be judges of these classes."

Rebecca Copus pictured after she won the grooming contest.

Marc Henrie.

REBECCA COPUS

Rebecca is nine years old and has been showing dogs since she was four. She has handled Hungarian Vizslas, Miniature Pinschers and a Dobermann. But as her parents breed Bearded Collies, this is the dog she is most familiar with.

"I always used to watch my mother when she was showing our dogs, and so I learnt a lot from her. I have also picked up a lot of hints by watching other handlers. I am interested in all aspects of working with dogs. In 1986 I was given a Miniature Pinscher but she had a bad shoulder and could not be shown. I started doing obedience work with her and I came first in a training class and was asked to do a demonstration at the Miniature Pinscher Club Championship Show. In 1988 I entered a Canine Triathlon where you had to groom a dog, do obedience work and finally take part in a canine quiz. It was great fun and I learnt a great deal. The next year I entered a grooming competition with one of our Bearded Collies. I spent two hours preparing her and I won the contest. I compete regularly in junior handling classes and I can hardly wait until I am given my very own Bearded Collie to show."

Julie Whiting specialises in handling Cocker Spaniels. Dave Freeman.

JULIE WHITING

Julie started competing in junior handling classes when she was ten years old and even then you could see she had a way with dogs. She qualified a total of thirty-two times for the semi-finals at Richmond and was awarded third place in 1984. The next year she finished in the last ten, in 1986 she was in the final six and in her last year as a junior she came third in the semi-finals. "My family breed Cocker Spaniels and I have won Best of Breed on a number of occasions," she said. "There is no doubt that the experience I gained as a junior has helped me in the breed ring. I am now judging junior handling classes at Open Shows."

AMY COWLARD

Amy started by taking the family pet Newfoundland to an Exemption Show and she won the junior handling class. "I caught the dog-showing bug and I longed to have my own dog to handle," said Amy, who is now twelve years old. "I was given a Miniature Poodle and joined the Mersham Ringcraft Club, where I learnt how to do things properly. I qualified for the semi-finals and made the final, where I finished third. I was nine years old and the youngest handler in the final.

Amy Cowlard shows Whippets and Standard Poodles.

"I now show Whippets as well as Poodles in breed classes, as well as competing in junior handling."

LYNDSAY PARKER

Lyndsay, who is now fourteen years old became involved in handling when her family bought a Boxer puppy to show.

"I was eleven years old at the time and I took our Boxer along to a training club. I made a lot of friends and started handling other breeds. One of the dogs was an English Setter called Valsett Principal Dancer (Arron) and I took him to Open Shows and competed in the breed classes and in junior handling.

"In 1987 I was offered a Bedlington Terrier called Bozen Bombshell (Harry) to handle on a permanent basis as the dog's owners could not travel to all the shows. We have formed a good

Lyndsay Parker with Valsett Principal Dancer.

Dave Freeman.

partnership and have qualified for Crufts and the Richmond semi-finals both years. In July 1988 I bought my own Bedlington Terrier, Bozen Barnaby (Oliver) and I spent most of the summer with the breeder learning about the care and grooming of the breed. I won a Reserve Challenge Certificate at the Midland Bedlington Terrier Club Show and a Challenge Certificate at Windsor Championship Show.

"I don't know how many times I have qualified for Richmond. I prefer the challenge of trying to qualify with several different breeds, rather than handling the same dog all the time."

GARY BROCKMAN

Gary Brockman specialises in showing English Bulldogs.

Gary has been competing in junior handling competitions for more than four years and has qualified for Richmond every year. He finished in the last eight, and then the last five. When he moved up to the twelve to sixteen age group he was again brought out into the final winning line-up. "I handle a variety of breeds from the Working Group and the Utility Group and I like handling the English Bulldog," he said.

LEANNE SMITH

Leanne Smith with Altricia Merc.

"I have been showing Rough Collies and Border Collies since I was seven years old and I have won at Championship and Open Shows, too," said Leanne. "I got interested because my grandmother owns the Altricia kennels and is also a handler."

Leanne was placed fifth in a class of seventy at the 1988 Richmond semi-finals. She was competing in the six-to-eleven age bracket in the Working group. She competes in breed competitions against adults and spends all her spare time helping to care for the dogs at her grandmother's kennels.

Nicole Burr and her Great Dane after competing at the Windsor Championship Show.

Lionel Young Photography.

NICOLE BURR

Nicole, aged sixteen, learnt to handle dogs at the Nailsworth Training Club. "I like to handle breeds in the Working Group because I think they present the biggest challenge," she said. "My favourite breed is the Great Dane, but my ambition is to handle a Scottish Terrier because of the difference in handling technique."

In 1988 Nicole competed in a class of one hundred entries in the twelve to sixteen class and she was placed second under judge Stewart Mallard. "I would count that as my most exciting win so far," said Nicole.

Kathryn Entwistle.

KATHRYN ENTWISTLE

"I have lived with dogs all my life, and when I was six I entered a junior handling class in Scotland with my parents' dog called Alpha," said Kathryn. "He was nearly bigger than me, but I managed to come second behind a girl who was much older than me. I am now twelve years old and I have won a lot of trophies, including the North West Canine Society's Child Handler of the Year in 1989. When I grow up I want to be a top handler in obedience."

Justine Waldron. She likes to do all the grooming and preparation for the dogs she shows.

Dalton.

JUSTINE WALDRON

"I started junior handling when I was ten years old and I was placed second at the Southern Counties Bearded Collie Club Championship Show. I had assumed it was just a matter of taking a dog into the ring, but I soon found out how wrong I was. It may look easy from the ringside, but it is a lot more difficult than it appears. I made a point of watching all the adult handlers, and the thing that impressed me most in the successful handlers was not only their rapport with the dog, but the co-ordination of movement that is required to match the dog. I was determined

Sarah Swigciski handles Cocker Spaniels and English Setters.

that I would achieve success in the ring, but I realised that it would mean a lot of practice and a lot of patience.

"It was soon after that that Toni Teasedale introduced me to Affenpinschers and I acquired one of my own – Tom Tiddler at Tonsarne. I was also still handling Beardies and I qualified several times for the JHA semi-finals. In 1987 Affenpinschers were classified at Crufts for the first time and naturally I took mine, as I had qualified. We achieved the absolute ultimate, winning Best of Breed at Crufts. Of course, that meant I had to handle my dog in the Toy Group with all the other Best of Breed winners. We had to enter the ring alphabetically, and so we had to lead the way in. I was the youngest Best of Breed handler and we got a lot of publicity.

"I regularly enter the junior handling classes in the club shows and I always like to do the finishing touches myself, making sure the dog has been properly groomed. Before going into the ring I like to try and establish a rapport with the dog and then I know it will give its best. After all, what dog will try its best for someone who has just picked up the lead?

"Junior handling is fiercely competitive and should not be dismissed as 'just for the kids'. I believe that many of the good future handlers will have worked their way through junior handling classes, and will have acquired an in-depth knowledge of their breed. I am now just out of the age limit for junior handling, but I feel I have learnt a lot from watching other juniors which will stand me in good stead for the future. I am currently campaigning a young puppy, and the experience I have gained through handling our dogs and other people's dogs is helping me get the best from her."

SARAH AND DAVID SWIGCISKI

Sarah and her brother David were brought up in a doggy family. Their father Peter was well known for his German Shepherd Dogs, but he has now switched to his wife's first loves, English Setters and Cocker Spaniels. Sarah and David both became involved in junior handling. David, with his workmanlike approach, preferred the Cocker Spaniels, and he won many classes at Open Show level and competed at the Richmond semi-finals on a number of occasions. Sarah started by handling a

David Swigciski. He often competed against his sister.

young English Setter bitch, Cosalta Orange Charade, and was soon winning in the younger age group. Several times brother and sister met, challenging each other as class winners, and usually Sarah came out on top. I met them on one of these occasions, and not knowing they were brother and sister, I asked the two class winners to swap dogs. No wonder they did well!

Sarah always had more grace and flair than David, and at the Richmond semi-finals she was placed second in a class of eighty. As David's enthusiasm waned, Sarah became increasingly involved in the show world and started handling Cocker Spaniels in the breed ring, but she preferred to handle English Setters in the junior handling classes.

"I handled Askann Clansman of Cosalta at Richmond and finished second," said Sarah. "The judge, Frank Lane, said it was a shame I wasn't a bit taller, as Clansman was a big dog to handle. I am now concentrating on Cocker Spaniels, and I strip them and prepare them for the show ring. I am now a full partner

Cathy Bennett in her junior handling days.

in my parents' kennels and I am starting to judge junior handling at Exemption and Open Shows."

CATHY BENNETT

"I started competing in junior handling when I was six years old with my parents' Afghan Hound called Zola. It was a wonder that I continued, because the dog had a habit of dragging me through a field of mud when it started raining. I would be flat out, hanging on to the lead for dear life, and then the dog would proceed to pull me out of the ring. My mother would yell at me: 'If you don't go back into the ring I won't take you to any more shows!' Things could only get better and I started achieving some success when I was given my own Saluki, named Star."

In the six years she was involved in junior handling Cathy qualified for the Richmond semi-finals sixty-three times. She competed in seven semi-finals and was placed second three times and third twice, and eventually won her class when she was fourteen years old. She also won the Treetops Shield, after winning over two hundred first prizes in events ranging from Exemption Shows to Championship Shows.

"My favourite part of competing is handling different breeds. I have handled twenty-five different breeds, and on the whole I have found the bigger dogs easier to cope with. Small dogs can be tricky. I also find it a challenge to handle nervous dogs and puppies, as it is very rewarding if you can overcome their nerves and get the best from them."

DONNA MCKENZIE

"From the earliest time I can remember I have always wanted to show dogs," said Donna. "We got our first dog, Kimmy, when I was two years old, and I went along to shows with my parents and my sister Lisa. As I was too young to show, I used to take a toy dog and pretend to show it in the ring after the judging had finished.

"When I was finally six years old, which seemed like a lifetime to me, my parents entered me in the junior handling classes at the London and Home Counties Boxer rally. I was the only junior in it, and Kimmy, now aged five, would not put his feet where I wanted them to go. I dropped the lead and ran to my Mum

Donna Mckenzie.with Kimmy and Little Dolly Daydream.

crying. Of course, I won a prize as there were no other juniors competing. After that, my Dad started coaching me and I started winning some of my classes.

"When I was nine years old I won the Treetops Shield for the first time. I had never even heard of the award and we had to ring up Liz Cartledge to find out what it was. Little did I realise I would win it for the next five years. The next dog I handled was Little Dolly Daydream, and with the help of my father we experimented with her and tried showing her free-standing rather than stacked. From that day I have always shown my dogs free-standing. I believe you can stand away from the dog and really show it off to its fullest potential.

"When I was twelve I started to get involved in breeding, and so I decided to cut down on junior handling classes and concentrate on the breed classes. In 1988 I won the Boscars Award organised by the British Boxer Club for the Best Junior Handler, and the following year I won my first Best of Breed with Dolly's half-brother Dexter. My ambition is start my own kennels with my Kimdon prefix, and I am hoping to qualify as a veterinary nurse."

James Cornell with Kortina's Big Bad Dom.

JAMES CORNELL

Basset Hounds are one of the most difficult dogs to show and it took James a lot of patience and determination to master the right technique. He joined the local Ringcraft club that specialised in junior handling, and he started off competing in Junior and Exemption Shows.

"In November my Basset Kortina's Big Bad Dom was born and I have worked very hard at training him," said James.

His efforts have paid off, for Big Bad Dom is now one of the most obedient Bassets in the show ring and has just been made a champion. In 1988 James qualified for the Richmond semi-finals and he reached the final eleven in the Hound Group.

LOUISE CORNELL

Louise is eleven years old and she also started showing the family Basset Hound.

"My first win came at an Exemption Show, when we won a class for the dog most like its owner. I put on a pair of furry ears from one of my toys! But I soon found that the Bassett was too heavy for me to handle in serious competition. I like breeds with long ears and short legs and so I now handle a Miniature Wire Haired Dachshund called Kizzy. He is a stubborn little thing, but he is improving all the time, and he is the right size for me."

CLAIRE SMITH
"I love the challenge of showing different breeds," said Claire. "I started handling an Old English Sheepdog called Tessa and I qualified for the 1987 Richmond semi-finals. Then my family rescued a Keeshound called Carla, and as it was difficult to handle I joined the Longlevens Dog Training Club. We went on to win the KCJO Open Stakes final at Birmingham Championship Show in 1989."

STEPHANIE PEARSON
Stephanie started exhibiting at Exemption Shows with Cocker Spaniels which is the breed that her mother campaigns. She started with Prince, who was just six months old, and trained at the Kennington Canine Society. She went on to handle a Dobermann and Great Danes. Then in 1988 she qualified for the Richmond semi-finals.

Stephanie Pearson.

"I was so nervous I kept making trips to the Ladies room," she said. "In fact, I almost missed my class!"

Fortunately her nerves settled down and Stephanie won the six to eleven year old class in the Gundog Group under judge Dr. Ron James. She went through to compete in the final at Birmingham and learnt a lot from the experience. In 1989 she moved up to the older age group but still managed to qualify ten times and was placed fifth in a class of eighty-three entries.

"My ambition is to win the Junior Handler of the Year, and then compete in the International Final at Crufts," she said.

Susan Crummy.

SUSAN CRUMMY

Susan is ten years old and started exhibiting in Junior Handling in 1988. "I compete in the six to eleven age group and I now show my Cocker Spaniel, called Darragh, in the breed classes," she said.

Susan Porter.

SUSAN PORTER

Susan is twelve years old and shows a Shih Tzu named Tashi. She has won a total of 130 rosettes in the two years she has been showing dogs.

PAULA JAYNE HILL

"I started handling dogs about four years ago with a Golden Retriever called Trudi. I now handle another Golden Retriever, called Ben, and I also show a couple of puppies. I go to the local training class, and I like going in for Obedience classes at the local shows. I have qualified for the Richmond semi-finals nine times, but I have not been able to compete as the date clashed with school term-time.

"My ambition is to become a dog beautician and to carry on handling dogs in the show ring."

EMMA FROST

" I first started handling nearly eleven years ago. I had a Norwegian Buhund, and I also used to handle other people's dogs. I used to practise and practise, but when I eventually qualified for the Richmond semi-finals, I was very nervous. I was dressed all in red to show off the dog, and I got through to the final six, out of a class of seventy. I qualified for Richmond for the next ten years, and my handling developed all the time. I have won some forty junior handling diplomas, and an award for the best ever handler of a Norwegian Buhund in obedience and in the show ring. I have now made up champions, and I trained our import Ch. Leitegards Kong Olaf Av Frostisen, who has now won

Emma Frost.

eight Challenge Certificates and five reserve Challenge Certificates.

"When you start handling, you have to work hard at learning all the different moves. You should be precise and confident in everything you do - and most important – don't get between the dog and the judge. I have found the more you watch other handlers, the more you learn. I think the handler's appearance also plays an important part. I dress in black and white, but mostly in red, in order to show off the dog. Remember the show ring etiquette and always be polite when the judge speaks to you.

"Junior handling is, above all, a fun thing to do. So, if you don't win, don't cry, and stamp your feet, and protest. Keep calm, smile, and go home and beat a pillow!"

Jan McMullan

JAN McMULLAN

"When I was about four years old, my Mum bought a Rough Collie called Chloe. My Mum didn't know how to show dogs so we went to ringcraft classes. We learnt how to stand and move Chloe and then we started to going to shows. I have won quite a lot of rosettes, and dog shows have become my great hobby."

HEATHER JOHNSON

Heather Johnson, aged 13, with Rawena.

"All my life I have wanted to own a dog, but my parents have never kept dogs. Every Christmas I used to hope that I would get a dog – but now at least I have a share in one. Dorothy Bridges, who runs the Longlevens ringcraft class asked me if I would like to train a Golden Retriever bitch called Rawena who was six months old. I jumped at the opportunity, but it wasn't as easy as I thought it would be. I had taken on a challenge because it is much harder to train a dog that doesn't belong to you. When we went to the ringcraft classes, Rawena kept pulling toward Miss Bridges. But slowly she began to gain confidence and was willing to co-operate with me. The big breakthrough came when I took her out for a run in a field. I called her and she came back to me. I knew then that I could take her where I wanted.

I enjoy going to shows, but I get annoyed when people who don't get a first or second storm out of the ring, muttering things about the judge. You can't expect to win all the time. Equally, you shouldn't love your dog because of what it wins – that isn't fair. The relationship you have with your dog is far more important than cups or rosettes.

Katherine Ham and Bonnie.

KATHERINE HAM

"I have always had dogs around me ever since I was very young; either on the farm or at home. I went to Crufts in 1987 and I looked at all the different breeds, and then read up on the dogs that I thought would fit in with my lifestyle. I eventually chose an Irish Setter, because they are an outdoors type of dog.

"I always wanted to show my dog, and when I won a fourth in a Best Condition class and a fifth in a puppy class, I was well and truly bitten by the show bug. Bonnie and I both loved showing, and we went to Exemption Shows nearly every week. It was at one of these shows that I got introduced to ringcraft classes. I made a silly mistake in a junior handling class. The lady who runs ringcraft pointed out my mistake and suggested that I went along to classes.

"Since then, Bonnie and I have done very well. I didn't realise there was so much to learn about showing. Bonnie's standing position and gait are so much better now. My relationship with her has also improved – we are now on the same wavelength and when we go to shows, Bonnie knows what is expected of her. In the last two years I have won four junior handling cups and about thirty rosettes. But winning isn't everything, even though it's nice when it happens. The most important thing is doing something well and, with the help of ringcraft classes, I have learnt a great deal.

VICTORIA ROSE

Victoria Rose

"It all started with a horse! Four years ago I was happily competing in the horse world when disaster struck. I had a fall and I had to undergo surgery on my leg. It took a while to recover and that meant the end of my career with horses. I was thirteen years old at the time, and after years of pleading, my parents finally allowed me to have a dog. We bought a West Highland White Terrier – Angilgate Twinkle, or Muppet as I call her – and I made my debut in the show ring. We went to many Open Shows, I read all the books I could find, and I attended ringcraft classes.

"My next dog was Heatherwood Heritage, known as Molly. She did well in the breed ring, but she excelled in the junior handling classes. We became a strong team, getting to the point when we could anticipate each other's moves. To achieve the highest standard you must know all the movements, mannerisms and actions, and give a polished performance. You need to find out what method of handling a judge likes, and exploit it to the full. You must be controlled and calm at all times. Be gentle, but firm with your dog and never allow it to misbehave in the ring. If you have trained and practised hard, this shouldn't happen very often, but dogs are not machines, and if a problem arises you must deal with it quickly and efficiently. You must be in charge.

"Sometimes you are asked to handle other dogs of different breeds or groups, and you must learn how to handle them. I have found the best way of doing this is by watching other breed classes, and pay particular attention if there are any professional handlers showing dogs."

Victoria's methods have certainly paid off. I have judged her on a number of occasions, and she has also been well placed by top professional handler such as Geoff Corish, Vince Mitchell and Albert Langley.

EMMA WILLIAMS

"I do not have a dog of my own but I have the loan of a Shih Tzu for shows," said Emma, aged thirteen. "It was very difficult to begin with because the dog kept looking towards its owner for instructions. One day I took him out for a walk so he would get to know him better. But when I let him off the lead he ran all the way home! Fortunately he is getting more used to me now and we won Best Tibetan Breed at the local Exemption Show."

CLAIRE HAMLETT

Claire is nine years old and first got interested in junior handling when her mother's Griffon Bruxellois had a litter of puppies and they kept three of them.

"I joined the special junior handling classes at Longlevens and I have also learnt a lot from going to shows with my mother," she said. She has won the junior handling class at the Griffon Bruxellois Championship Show and was the best child handler in the younger age group at the Gloucestershire Exemption Show.

Chapter Thirteen

JUNIOR HANDLING ABROAD

Junior handling has increased enormously in popularity since those early days in the Thirties when the first Junior Showmanship competition was staged in the United States. Today some eighteen countries compete in the International Junior Handler final at Crufts, and the numbers are growing every year. The standard has become very high, and the juniors competing at this level are usually destined for a career in the show world.

Each country has its own rules and regulations for junior handling competitions, and ring procedures may also vary. But although the process of qualifying for the International Final differs, the stages of elimination ensure that each country is represented by its top junior handler, who will be able to perform all the procedures that are required at the Crufts final.

UNITED STATES OF AMERICA

This is the original home of competitions for junior handlers, and the States has been well represented in the International Final by Clint Livingstone, who is now a fully fledged professional handler. He won the competition outright in 1988.

Junior Showmanship, as it is known in America, is organised in conjunction with the American Kennel Club and the competitions are carefully controlled by a series of regulations and guidelines. These are tremendously useful as a guide for juniors who are starting off in competition, and equally for the judges of junior handling classes. The judges, who must have suitable qualifications in this area, know exactly what is expected of them. This is a procedure that I would very much like to see adopted in Britain, and all other countries where junior handling classes are staged.

The American Kennel Club Guide
To Junior Showmanship Competition
For Juniors

1. Juniors are important to the sport of dogs. Juniors who learn about good sportsmanship, dogs, handling and dog shows will be valuable to the sport in the future. Junior Showmanship classes are offered at most dog shows. These classes are held so that young people can:
a. Experience winning and losing among those who are similar in age.
b. Learn the correct way to handle the breed they own.
c. Practice handling skills in competition.
d. Improve the way they handle their own dog.
e. Prepare for handling a dog in the regular classes.
2. Junior Showmanship classes are judged on the ability of the junior to handle his or her dog. The quality of the dog is not judged. Juniors will be asked to demonstrate:
a. Moving their dog with the rest of the class.
b. Presenting their dog in the standing position proper for its breed (including the use of an examining table for those breeds

normally judged on a table.)
c. Moving the dog individually in a regular pattern.
3. Juniors are expected to know basic ring routines. They should be able to follow directions, use space wisely, and be familiar with gaiting patterns. Juniors should appear "ring wise," alert to what is going on in the ring, and should be prepared for changes in the routine of judging.

JUNIORS MUST BE ABLE TO CONTROL THEIR DOGS AT ALL TIMES. Any junior who cannot control his or her dog will be excused by the judge.
4. Appearance and Conduct. Juniors should be clean, neat, and well-groomed. They should wear clothing that is comfortable to handle in and appropriate for dog shows. Clothing should not distract nor limit or hinder the judge's view of the dog.

Dogs should be groomed and trimmed as they would be for the breed ring. Judges will not evaluate the quality of the grooming and trimming, but juniors should make an effort to prepare their dogs for the ring. Unnecessary grooming of the dog in the ring to gain attention is not proper conduct.

Juniors should appear confident, prepared, business-like and attentive. They should be courteous to both the judge and other juniors. Juniors are expected to handle their dogs without disturbing the dogs of the other juniors. Juniors should not crowd and they should not disturb others by continued use of toys and bait. Juniors should be alert to the needs of their dogs. They should use firm but thoughtful hands in controlling and handling their dogs. Juniors should not be impatient or heavy-handed.
5. Juniors will be judged on their ability to present their dogs in the same way the dog is properly handled in the breed ring. Juniors will also be judged on their ability to make their individual dog look its best both in pose and motion. During all parts of the competition juniors should handle their dogs in a quiet, smooth, efficient manner. Juniors should strive to make the dog stand out as the most important part of the team effort.
6. Junior handlers should:
a. Keep their dog's attention without using dramatic or unnecessary movements.
b. Gait their dogs in a controlled trot without distracting or

interfering with the judge's view of the dog. Be aware of what is going on in the ring.
c. Concentrate on their dog and not the judge.
d. Junior handlers who use exaggerated posture, motions or gestures in any part of the competition will be faulted.
7. There are many ways juniors can find help in learning about Junior Showmanship and handling their own dogs. In addition to the help of parents, juniors may seek the advice of experienced breeder-exhibitors, professional handlers, handling instructors, and former juniors. They may also learn from the AKC breed video cassettes, books on handling, books on individual breeds, and observing breed and group judging at dog shows.

Junior Showmanship
Judging Guidelines

1. DEFINITION AND PURPOSE: Junior Showmanship classes are non-regular classes which are judged solely on the ability and skill of juniors in handling their dogs as in the breed ring. The purpose of Junior Showmanship Competition is two-fold: to introduce and encourage juniors to participate in the sport of dogs; and to provide juniors with a meaningful competition in which they can learn, practice, and improve in all areas of handling skill and sportsmanship. It is important that judges of Junior Showmanship Competition understand the definition and purpose of these classes and take seriously their role in guiding the future guardians of the sport. JUDGES ARE EXPECTED TO HAVE A GENUINE INTEREST IN JUNIORS AND IN JUNIOR SHOWMANSHIP COMPETITION.
2. PRE-REQUISITES FOR JUDGES: Those who judge Junior Showmanship must be familiar with the Junior Showmanship Rules and Regulations as well as all other rules and policies that apply to all judges. Many of the guidelines outlined previously in The Guidelines for Dog Show Judges have application to judging Junior Showmanship. It is therefore imperative that all those who judge Junior Showmanship be thoroughly versed in these areas.

Judges shall have completed all provisional requirements for Breed or Junior Showmanship. They shall have demonstrated successfully their ability to conduct their ring in a consistent, business-like and safe manner that will instil confidence in exhibitors and spectators. Those person who have had previous experience in handling their own dogs successfully as well as those with experience as professionals are particularly encouraged to apply and become qualified for this important part of the sport.

3. RESPONSIBILITIES FOR JUNIOR SHOWMANSHIP JUDGES: It is important for judges to be teachers by example. They should be prompt, courteous, patient and properly attired. Judges must be impartial and totally separate the handling ability of the juniors they judge from any other consideration. From the exhibitor's point of view impartiality extends to eliminating from the judging process bias for or against the breed handled, any thought of past or future assignments, friendships, external knowledge of a junior's record of competition, or prior knowledge or assumption of the dog's training or preparation.

Judges should never solicit or offer to judge Junior Showmanship. If asked by a show-giving club to judge, acceptance should be based on whether or not they feel capable of judging juniors.

4. SAFETY: Juniors with varying degrees of experience and dogs with great difference in size, temperament and training need safe ring conditions. Judges must make every effort to ensure the safety of the juniors and their dogs during competition. Judges should arrange or rearrange competitors in order of gaiting speed or size of dog to avoid crowding and instruct juniors to leave space for judging between themselves and the junior in front of or behind them. Moving two dogs together (side by side) is discouraged as is any pattern which places any dog in close proximity to other dogs when lead control is at a minimum, i.e. on a loose lead, etc. In large classes judges should admit only as many juniors into the ring as can be safely examined. Never hesitate to divide any class for any reason where the safety of the individuals or the dogs is involved. Likewise do not hesitate to excuse any dog from the ring which is out of control, lame or which is otherwise ineligible to complete. Any dog showing signs of viciousness should be excused immediately. SAFETY IN THE JUNIOR SHOWMANSHIP RING CANNOT BE OVER-EMPHASIZED AND IT IS THE RESPONSIBILITY OF

THE JUDGE TO CONTROL HIS RING IN SUCH A MANNER THAT ANY ACTION BY A DOG OR HANDLER CANNOT COMPROMISE THE SAFETY OF THE RING.

The determination of safe conditions, excusals, etc. are solely the judge's decisions, and should be rendered by the judge without consultation.

5. JUDGING ROUTINE: The actual routine of judging will vary according to the judge, the number of juniors, size of the ring, ring conditions, weather and time of day. However, judges should strive to evaluate competitors in an appropriate and consistent manner. It is very important that only those procedures and patterns of gaiting commonly used in regular dog show classes be used. The judge should be aware of the different breeds he will see in the ring and the particular ways in which these breeds are normally handled. Examining tables shall be used only for breeds that are normally examined on a table. Although the procedure for completing the examination of the dogs should closely resemble that of breed judging, examination of the dogs for Junior Showmanship can be done rapidly because the conformation of the dog is of no concern. Judges should be consistent in the initial examination of each junior using the same gaiting patterns, the same procedural requests and allow each junior approximately the same amount of time.

However, judges may change the examining routine when making a further appraisal of selected competitors. A judge should not confuse the ability of a junior to take directions with the Junior's ability to handle his dog. Some freedom of expression and expertise should be allowed. To have all exhibitors handle as if by rote defeats the basic premise of Junior "SHOWMANSHIP".

Judges should consider how their own movements in the ring may precipitate awkward and unusual handling results. For example: when examining the class as a whole in motion, the judge should be inside the circle; and when examining a class of standing or posed dogs the judge should not move from one side of the line to the other creating unnecessary handling movements.

Judges should limit conversation with juniors during competition to that which is absolutely necessary and UNDER

NO CIRCUMSTANCES SHOULD QUESTIONS BE USED AS A MEANS OF TESTING A JUNIOR'S KNOWLEDGE.

6. JUDGE'S EXAMINATION AND EVALUATION: The judge should examine and evaluate the class of juniors in four basic areas: proper breed presentation, knowledge of ring procedures and appearance and conduct. The general rule in evaluating a handler's capabilities is ECONOMY OF MOTION. Handlers who use exaggerated motions and gestures in any phase of their presentation of the dog should be faulted. In essence, the judge should hardly be aware of the capable handler's presence while completing the dog's examination. In many respects a Junior Showmanship judge's principal consideration should be to find those juniors who possess a "hand for dogs". Those handlers having this attribute neither over nor under handle their dogs. They present their dogs in a quiet, efficient manner. They are able to keep their dog's attention without dramatic or unnatural movements. They are able to gait their dogs in a collected trot, never distracting or interfering with the judge's vision of the dog.

BREED PRESENTATION. While the judge must consider all areas important in evaluating the overall capabilities of juniors, it is doubly important that the junior present his dog in the proper manner for the breed being handled and that the judge is cognizant of the proper presentation of that breed. It is imperative therefore that the judge should have prior knowledge of the breeds which are to be presented and that they familiarize themselves with the proper ways of handling those breeds. If the Show Superintendent or Show Secretary does not furnish a list of those breeds in the Judging Programme then the judge should request the list well in advance of the show date. In the individual presentation of the dog the junior should demonstrate the ability to handle the dog as it is handled in the breed ring, showing the dog to its best advantage in pose and in motion. During all phases of handling the junior's concentration should be on the dog and not on the judge but not to the extent that he/she is unaware of what is taking place in the ring. Remember you are judging the handler, but time should be spent looking at the dog to gain insight as to how well it is being handled.

1. Is the dog responsive to the handler? Do they work as a team?
2. Does the dog appear posed or interested at all times?

3. Is the dog under control?
4. Is the dog moved correctly and to the best of its ability?
5. Are the dog's main faults being minimized?
6. Do both the dog and handler appear relaxed?
7. Is the dog presented with an apparent minimum effort?

KNOWLEDGE OF RING PROCEDURE. The judge shall evaluate the ability of the junior to follow directions, use space wisely, and execute the requested gaiting patterns. Juniors should appear "Ring Wise," alert to the judging progression and be prepared for changes to the judging routine.

APPEARANCE AND CONDUCT. The judge should be aware of the appearance of both the handler and the dog. The junior should be suitably dressed for the occasion wearing clothing that will not hinder or detract from the presentation of the dog. The dog would be groomed and trimmed in the manner associated with the breed. However, the judge should not evaluate either the dress of the handler nor the grooming of the dog, but rather that an effort has been made. Excessive grooming of the dog in the ring to gain the judge's attention is inappropriate and should be faulted accordingly.

The judge shall evaluate the general conduct of juniors in the ring. Juniors should appear prepared, confident, business-like and attentive. They should be courteous to both the judge and their fellow exhibitors. Juniors are expected to handle their dogs without distracting the dogs of other competitors. A junior who crowds or disturbs other dogs should be faulted. A principle of Junior Showmanship is to afford the opportunity to learn the spirit of competition. Winning is important but is secondary to development of sportsmanship in competition. Judges who reward unsportsmanlike conduct or actions, regardless of a handler's other capabilities, compromise the very premise of Junior Showmanship.

Juniors should be alert to the needs of their dogs, realizing the welfare of their dog is important. They are responsible for the control of their dogs at all times. However, juniors who exhibit impatience or heavy-handedness with their dogs should be penalized.

Clint Livingstone: International Junior Handler of the Year in 1988.

Petrulis

CLINT LIVINGSTONE

Clint comes from a doggy family. His parents have been involved in dogs for well over twenty years, in the show ring and in obedience trials. In 1972 they opened their own kennels with boarding and training facilities, so Clint grew up living and breathing dogs. He first started showing dogs when he was seven years old, and by the time he was fifteen he was helping out the professional handlers at shows, who sometimes handle up to twenty dogs. In the past two years he has attended over three hundred shows, and in all, he has been to dog shows in thirty-two states in America.

In 1985 and 1986 he was the top German Shepherd Dog junior handler, and was also the number one handler in the Herding

Group in 1986. In 1987 Clint competed in junior showmanship classes with a Golden Retriever and an English Pointer, and in the overall competition he was 100 points ahead of all the other handlers, which was the greatest winning margin in the history of the competition. This entitled him to an all-expenses-paid trip to London to compete for the international title at Crufts, which he went on to win.

"One of my greatest achievements was winning the International Junior Handler of the Year in 1988," said Clint. "The competition was truly exhilarating. Princess Antoinette of Monaco was there to present the cup, and the photographers were everywhere. I was on television – it was an amazing experience. The junior handler title had not been won by the USA for five years, and now I was the top junior handler in the world.

"I have had a wonderful chance to travel through junior handling, and I have met a lot of interesting people. It also helped me to decide on my future career of veterinary medicine."

In January 1989 Clint became a professional handler, and has been very successful both in the breed ring and in the Groups. He is currently studying for his college degree, but he plans to remain active in the show world.

AUSTRALIA

Australia have finished in the final six of the International Final for the past three years and in 1987 Simon Briggs won the title. The following year Tabitha Buckley came third.

The Junior Handling Competition is conducted by affiliated clubs of the member bodies of the Australian National Kennel Council. The winner of the PAL Junior Showmanship Competition is invited to attend Crufts to compete for the International Junior Handlers Final. The ring procedure varies slightly from the British format and competitors are judged on a points system.

HANDLING PROCEDURE

1. Entrants will be required to parade their dogs on the LEFT hand side.
2. Dogs must be brought to the judge and posed to their best advantage.
3. Dogs must be moved from, and back to, the judge as requested.
4. The aim is for handlers to control and exhibit their charges.

EXERCISES

UP AND BACK

With the dog in the LEFT HAND ALL THE TIME, move up to the ring edge directly in front of you. Turn so the dog turns on the INSIDE.
Return to the Judge, set your dog up.

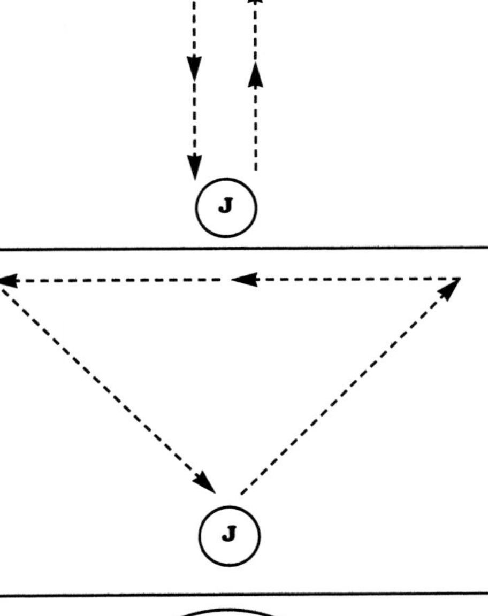

CORRECT TRIANGLE

Start with the dog in the LEFT HAND and move to your right-hand top side of the ring. Now move across to the other top-side and return directly to the judge. Set your dog up.

"O" PATTERN (or Around the Ring)

Simplest of all! Start with the dog in your LEFT HAND, move anti-clockwise and finish where you started. Set your dog up.

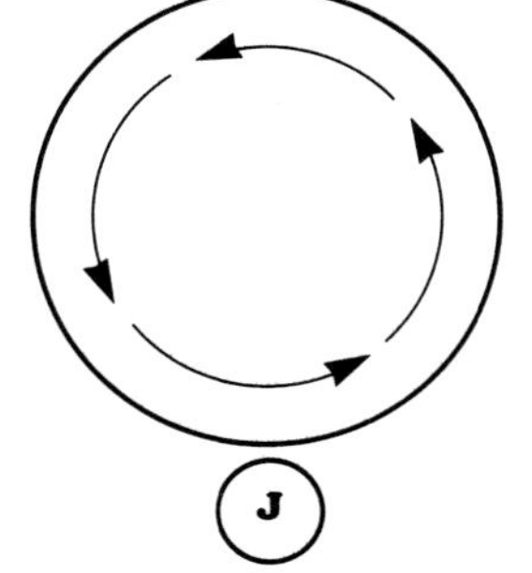

JUDGING

70 points for correct handling, exhibition and presentation of the dog.
15 points for the handler's attire, having regard to its harmony with the exhibit.
15 points for the preparation, bloom and presentation of the dog.
The judges and stewards require dogs to be paraded and moved around the ring in the same manner or pattern as that required in an ordinary show competition. The normal triangular course is recommended. Unorthodox movements or attempts to confuse or trick the handler must be discouraged.

Fancy dress, or other attire that is unsuited to the efficient exhibition of dogs must be penalised severely; and in coming to a final decision, if the foregoing rules are kept firmly in mind, the judges should eventually select the handler who is best equipped to handle a good dog in open competition.

NEW ZEALAND

Junior Handling is becoming increasingly popular in New Zealand and in the three years they have been represented, they have finished in the final six. Their best result to date was in 1988 when Johanna Vos, of the famous Clan-Abby Kennels, was the runner-up.

All clubs in New Zealand are entitled to hold a junior handling class in conjunction with a Championship Show. The New Zealand Kennel Club hold these classes at the Tux National Dog Show and the Champ Classic Shows. The regulations and ring procedure is run on the same format as junior handling classes in Australia, and they are also judged on a points system.

The representative for the International Final is selected at the Pal Junior Handler Competition. This is a separate competition held under separate regulations by the New Zealand Kennel Club. Ten heats are held in October and November – three in the north of the North Island, three in the south of the North Island, and four in the South Island. The final is held in mid-Novemeber as a special event in conjunction with a Championship Show. The

Johanna Vos: Runner-up in the 1988 International Handler of the Year, pictured with Clan-Abby Phantom of Love, New Zealand Ch. Lochiel-Loire at Clan-Abby and Aust/N.Z. Ch. Casanova's Joy of Clan-Abby.

venue is Wellington, Auckland or Christchurch, on a rotating basis and the ten finalists are flown to the venue to compete in the final. Pal Dog Food offers very generous sponsorship and the first prize is a trip for two to London to compete in the International Final.

JOHANNA VOS

Joahnna started handling dogs in the junior handling ring when she was five years old, and even then she showed she had a special gift for working with animals.

"I used to dress my dogs up as if they were dolls," said Joanna. "But I soon started to get more serious about handling dogs. I have been showing dogs in the breed ring since I was twelve years old, and I always like to train the dog myself."

Johanna has mostly worked with the four types of collie, in particular with Border Collies. She now plays a very important part in maintaining the success of her parents' Border Collie kennels. She trains the dogs to a very high standard and is well known for her handling skills in the breed ring.

IRELAND

Ireland supplies regular representatives to the International Final and I particularly remember Andrea Bollard who I judged in 1989. She had a calm and cheerful manner and it seemed that nothing could upstage her. She appeared to enjoy the day to the full and gave an excellent demonstration of her skills. In 1990 it was Monica Boardman's turn to represent her country, and she brought a lot of experience to the occasion.

The Irish Junior Handling Club was established in 1982, and they have about fifty members. Three adults are elected to the posts of Chairman,Treasurer and Secretary and they offer help and advice to the junior competitors. They are currently in the process of setting up training classes, as some of the members were struggling with the ring procedure. The classes are separated into three age groups: ten to twelve years, thirteen to fifteen years, and sixteen to eighteen years. The classes are judged on a point system, and a total of ten points are required in order to qualify for the Irish Final. Four points are awarded towards a first prize, three points towards a second prize, two points towards a third prize and one point towards a fourth prize.

There are fifteen qualifying shows throughout the year where points are available. Usually the procedure at the final is that all the handlers enter the ring and compete against each other, and the judge would choose his winning line-up in order of first, second, third and fourth. But in the 1989 final, they competed according to age group, and the judge selected the first four in each age group. Then the winners from each age group competed against each other to find the Irish Junior Handler of the Year, who qualified for the International Final at Crufts.

MONICA BOARDMAN

Monica is seventeen years old and comes from County Dublin, Ireland. She won the final in her country and was declared Junior Handler of the Year, qualifying to represent Ireland in the International Junior Handling Finals at Crufts 1990.

"I handle Dalmatians and Japanese Spitz and have been competing in junior handling classes for eight years," said Monica.

Monica Boardman: Ireland's Junior Handler of the Year in 1989.

MALTA

Tony Portelli was the first junior to represent his country in 1989 and I was impressed by the positive way in which he approached his task. I selected him for my final six. The following year Jeffry Micalef did a fine job and was a credit to his country. For such a small country, Malta produces some very good handlers.

Junior Handlers are selected to compete at the International Final at Crufts by the following procedures:

1. Entrants first compete with their own dog and they are assessed accordingly.
2. The handlers are numbered from one to ten. The handler of the first number to be drawn changes his dog with the handler of the second number drawn. For example, if numbers two and seven

are drawn, those two handlers exchange dogs.
3. All handlers with different dogs are given five minutes to practise with their new dog outside the ring where the main event is being held.
4. The ten handlers enter the ring with their new dogs, and after going through their procedures, they return with their own dogs. Finally the judge chooses the four best handlers.
5. The competition is based on a points system. The winner is given four points, the runner-up is given three points, the third two points and the fourth one point. The handler who gets the highest number of points at the end of the year is entitled to take part in the International Junior Handler competition held at Crufts.

SPAIN

MARIA JOSE HARO

Maria Jose Haro: She represented Spain in the 1989 International Final.

Maria Jose, who comes from Spain, is carrying on the family tradition and is the fourth generation to own and show English Pointers. Her great grandfather owned Pointers in 1920 and the breed has been part of the family ever since.

"I learnt to say 'Tosca' (the name of their bitch) before I could say Mama or Papa," said Maria Jose.

She accompanied her parents to all the shows and when she was three years old she exhibited her own Pointer, Spinner of

Crookrise. She won her first junior handling class when she was five, and when she competed at the Malaga shows she won the junior handling class in three consecutive years. In 1988 she won the national competition in Madrid and so she qualified for the 1989 International Final when she was only eleven years old. I judged her and thought she was very good for someone who was still very young. She is now learning how to handle an Afghan Hound.

SWEDEN

Sweden has sent over some outstanding representatives for the International Final and as a result they have won the competition in two successive years. Lena Ekbom took honours in 1989 and the following year Pernilla Wistead also won the event.

Sweden has ten international shows every year in all parts of the country starting from February through to November. At each of these shows junior handling competitions are held for youngsters aged between ten and sixteen years old. The national finals are held in Stockholm in December, at Scandinavia's most prestigious dog show. About eighty young handlers take part and the winner is chosen to represent Sweden at the International Junior Handlers Final at Crufts.

LENA EKBOM

Lena is now sixteen years old. She grew up with dogs and has been handling them since she was nine. Her mother breeds West Highland White Terriers and Lena owns a Flat Coat Retriever.

"I came to England for a year to help Mrs Hands of the Crinan Kennels with her Westies," said Lena. "This gave me the opportunity to compete in junior handling classes. I qualified for the semi-finals and won the Terrier Group, but I did not compete in the final. I had also won the Swedish final and so I decided to represent my country."

This was the year that I judged the International final, and I made Lena my winner. She remained calm and composed throughout the competition and demonstrated her skills to perfection.

Following her win at Crufts she judged junior handling at the prestigious Windsor Championship Show and she has also judged in Sweden and Germany.

"My chief interest is now in Salukis, but I also hope to carry on judging junior handling," said Lena.

DENMARK

Michael Christiansen has represented his country in the International Final three times. The junior handling competition takes place at the Danish Kennel Klub's International Championship Shows every year. Competitors must be aged between ten years old and sixteen. But anyone who qualifies for the semi-finals and reaches the age of seventeen before the start of the competition is still allowed to enter.

Finland, Norway, West Germany, Canada, Holland, Portugal, Singapore, Monaco and Belgium are all represented at Crufts. Deep down, each individual wants to win the coveted title International Junior Handler of the Year, yet in my experience all the competitors have demonstrated good sportsmanship while they are competing in the ring. This has added greatly to the enjoyment of the competition and it is now a highspot of the world's greatest dog show.

APPENDICES

I

GLOSSARY OF TERMS

Judges use a number of technical terms in the show ring, and juniors should make sure they are familiar with them before entering a competition.

STANCE, POSE IT, STACK IT: These can all be used when the judge is asking the handler to pose the dog for examination.
STAND, STAND NATURALLY, NATURAL POSE: The handler should position the dog without touching it. The dog should be allowed to walk into the position that is normal to that breed.
WINDY: Nervous, shy, apprehensive.
GAIT IT, MOVE IT: Instruction to walk or run your dog in order for the judge to evaluate its soundness on the move.
UP AND BACK, UP AND DOWN, TO THE CORNER: Move or gait your dog away from the judge to a section of the ring designated by the judge, then return at the same speed directly towards the judge in a straight line.
TRIANGLE: Move your dog in the shape of a triangle.
COME OUT, I'M NOT PLACING YOU, I'LL HAVE YOU OUT: The judge wants to reassess the handler prior to making a final decision for his winners. He wants you to stand in the centre of the ring with the other handlers.

TEETH, BITE, MOUTH: The judge wants to look at the dog's dentition in order to see if the teeth meet properly, and to check if it has a full set of teeth.
CRABBING: The dog is going forward with a side movement like a crab. This should be corrected.
PACING: The dog is not reaching out in a smooth stride; the front leg and rear leg on the same side are both doing the same movement.
PIN-TOEING, TOEING OUT: The dog is walking towards the judge with unsound action, usually out at elbow, suggesting a criss-crossing pattern.
EAST-WEST STANCE, TEN-TO-TWO STANCE: The dog is being allowed to stand with its feet turned out, looking as if it is weak in pastern. A little correction will usually alter this, plus more road-walking on the lead to strengthen the muscle.
OVER-REACHING: The dog is stretched out too far at the rear.
ROCKING-HORSE STANCE: Legs too far in front and stretched out too far at rear.
AMBLING: This is allowed in some large breeds.
NATURAL GAIT: Well-constructed dogs have a natural gait.
TROT: Sometimes seen in the movement of terriers.
SINGLE TRACKING: All the footprints falling on a single line of travel.

II

JUNIOR HANDLING ASSOCIATIONS

Mrs Liz Cartledge,
Ryslip Kennels,
Binfield Park,
Bracknell,
Berks.
Telephone: 0344 424144

Irish Junior Handling Association,
Monica Boardman,
Portrane Road,
Donabate,
County Dublin.
Telephone: 0001 436270

III

JUNIOR HANDLING CLASSES

There are dog training clubs and societies throughout the country, and a number now hold classes for junior handlers.

East Surrey Ringcraft Association,
United Refoirm Church Hall,
Harestone Valley Road,
Caterham,
Surrey.
Contact Mrs Pat Brigden. Telephone: 0883 342274
Tuesday evening, just before the adult classes, which begin at 8pm.

Doncaster Canine Society,
Social Club of the R.L. Football Club,
Bentley Road,
Doncaster.
(On the A19 Doncaster to Selby Road).
Contact Mrs Maureen Oliver. Telephone: 0302 855280
Every second Tuesday, 7.30-9pm.

North Dorset All-Breeds Training Club,
Manston Village Hall,
Manston,

Dorset.
Contact Mrs Kerry Frost. Telephone: 0747 811818
Every Thursday, 7-9pm.

Oundle and Distict Dog Training Club,
The Victoria Hall,
Oundle
Contact Mrs Hilary Hannah. Telephone: 08015-678
Every Monday, 8pm-10pm.

Fleet and District Dog Training Society,
Crondall Village Hall,
Nr. Farnham,
Surrey.
Contact Mrs Pam Morton. Telephone: 0256 862747
First Thursday in the month.

Longlevens Ringcraft Training
Longlevens Community Centre,
Church Road,
Longlevens,
Gloucs.
Contact Miss Dorothy Bridge. Telephone: 0452 23912
Every Monday 7.30-9pm.

The Yorkshire Junior Handling Association,
29 Spink Hall Lane,
Stocksbridge,
Sheffield,
Contact Mrs Lynda Barnes. Telephone: 0742 884209
Mrs Alice Scanlon. Telephone: 0274 488165

Cavendish Ringcraft Training,
St Olive Church Hall,
Woodberry Down,
London N4.
Contact Frank or Gloria. Telephone: 071- 272 8069